The author, born in South Yorkshire in 1938, was an early pioneer of paid continental cycle racing. He then established a successful career in financial services. Currently, he was a reluctant rider at the outset of the professional class in the UK. Then he organised the most successful cycle training camps in Mallorca for 20 years. He became a permanent resident in France in 2005, also having winter homes in the Algarve & Mallorca, consequently having considerable travel, racing & club experiences in those & other countries including South Africa, winning a world championship in Russia.

Gordon Neale

Cycling 70 Years: Once World Champion

AUSTIN MACAULEY PUBLISHERS™
LONDON • CAMBRIDGE • NEW YORK • SHARJAH

Copyright © Gordon Neale 2023

The right of Gordon Neale to be identified as author of this work has been asserted by the author in accordance with sections 77 and 78 of the Copyright, Designs and Patents Act 1988.

All rights reserved. No part of this publication may be reproduced, stored in a retrieval system, or transmitted in any form or by any means, electronic, mechanical, photocopying, recording, or otherwise, without the prior permission of the publishers.

Any person who commits any unauthorised act in relation to this publication may be liable to criminal prosecution and civil claims for damages.

This is a work of fiction. Names, characters, businesses, places, events, locales, and incidents are either the products of the author's imagination or used in a fictitious manner. Any resemblance to actual persons, living or dead, or actual events is purely coincidental.

A CIP catalogue record for this title is available from the British Library.

ISBN 9781398486089 (Paperback)
ISBN 9781398486096 (ePub e-book)

www.austinmacauley.com

First Published 2023
Austin Macauley Publishers Ltd®
1 Canada Square
Canary Wharf
London
E14 5AA

I would like to acknowledge the contribution of my father, Norman Joshua Neale, born in 1909 affectionately known as "Joshe" to his friends, for my introduction to cycling at a young age and his contribution as secretary to my first club, Mexborough Road club. The support I received over many years from my first wife, Janet, should not be underestimated, as she said, she married a cyclist, and nothing would change that. Unfortunately, she contracted legionnaires in Mallorca, in 2008, which largely contributed to her early death. My thanks also go to my second wife, Phyllis, for her design of this book cover. Of origin American she studied fine arts in Iowa, Chicago and New York, subsequently exhibiting extensively in Europe.

Last but not least, this book is a dedication and memorial to the characters including my father, living and deceased, that have made the cycling community all the richer.

Table of Contents

St Brieuc to Barcelona and Tarragonna	14
Following Tom Simpson to St Brieuc 1960	20
Father and Father's Trip to France	24
1960 Continued Racing in St Brieuc	27
London 1960/61 and UK Before 1960	38
Club Life Before 1960	44
Second Year in France 1961	49
Tour De France L'avenir 1961	56
Mid Auot Bretagne 1961	62
Amateur Road Racing and Tom Simpson Before 1960	67
Third Year in France 1962	73
End of Year in Brittany 1962 and Now Back to UK	80
Back from France: Now Home for Good?	83

Looking for Work and New Professional Racing Licenses	85
Pro Race Isle of Man and Tom Simpson's Demise	90
Starting in Business 1970	96
Bike Out Again Sad Death Pat Bradley	99
Meeting Georges in Canada and Florida	102
Joined Doncaster Wheelers Starting 1978	106
1978 + First Races South of France	112
Travel Agency Purchase and Business Expansion	116
Training Camps in Mallorca	119
Training Camp Continue Finding Your Way	124
Training Camps Mallorca Bill Cheadle, Personalities and Nicknames	130
Training Camp Continued The Good, the Bad and the Ugly	135
Names for Places	142
Hazards and Accidents	145
Seniors Having Fun	155
Tour of Luxembourg	157
Tour De Mallorca	161
Buying Property in France 1990	167

Tour of Bavaria (Bayern Rundfahrt) June 1987	**170**
France Cyclo Sportives Discovered	**177**
Peter Fryer Trophy Series	**182**
Mountain Biking	**185**
Russian World Road Race Championship for Veterans	**187**
Investec Stage Race South Africa 1993	**198**
Dinnington Club Life	**202**
Klagenfurt Tourist Games, Deutschlondsberg and St Johann Austria	**207**
No More Racing	**213**
Cyclo-Tourists in Brittany	**215**
Winter Riding in Portugal's Algarve	**224**
Cyclos Pilgrimage to Fatima	**227**
Nuts and Bolts	**234**

Its Black Friday 13th March 2020, I made a mental note, perhaps I will have the time to write that book that my friends had often suggested I write. Why? Today my fiancé Phyllis and I had just spoken to Pam, a New York friend of Phyllis, that came to visit us here in Portugal this January. She told us she was sick with a bad cough, everyone was coughing in her office, even the boss's daughter, who he would not let go home, with all the covid 19 pandemic in the rest of the world we knew it had arrived in New York, even if they did not.

Today is the 17th of April, Phyllis and I are still in Tavira, Portugal, we only come here in the winter, going back home to Plouha, Cotes de Goello, on the coast in Brittany, France after our winter sojourn. It is here where I have been paying my taxes for the French government to misspend, since 2005. Fortunately, I have the luxury of being able to ride my bike alone, unlike my French clubmates who are locked in. Phyllis, who is an artist, is happy doing her paintings in the garden, she is currently painting a series of Portuguese wells, (Nora's in Portuguese) that as far as we are aware, has not been done before. They date back to when the Muslims occupied the Iberian Peninsula and are rapidly disappearing. She is a professional artist, born in Des Moines USA, now with dual French American citizenship. So, all in all we are better staying here for the moment, we are likely to be here for some time, whether we like it or not. Today I have started to put pen to paper, where better to start than with my arrival in Saint Brieuc, Brittany France, to ride my bike, courtesy of Tom Simpson. Who at the time I thought was being a good friend, latter I had my doubts? Like Tom, I thought I could be better occupied riding my bike, than being paid 25 shillings per week for marching up and down.

Swinton, South Yorkshire where I was born and lived is the home of Rockingham Cycling club, some would say more famously the Rockingham pottery. At that time the epicentre of the coal mining industry. All my friends who were nearing National Service age, suddenly obtained jobs as plumbers, electrician, fitters etc, to join the rest of their family working in the mines. There was only one person that I knew of, from our area that actually went to do his national service, I went to his wedding. Later he went off to do his service, leaving a wife & young baby behind, the reward he received after his 2 years were up, was his service was extended a further 6 months for some emergency or other. I believe this extended to a further year. Tom also came from a mining family, 15 miles away from me at Harworth, North Nottinghamshire. Which was why apart from cycling we knew one another.

It was a typical January day when I arrived at the Murphy household in Saint Brieuc, where Tom had arranged for me to stay. My immediate impressions of the town on the way from the railway station, was the lack of pavements (sidewalks), which was strange coming from the UK. This gave an air of neglect, which was otherwise false. The house was situated on the Rue de Rennes, with a shop attached. This was a good clue to Monsieur Murphy Snr's occupation as a butcher, he also worked at the local abattoir. The road continued to the east with a long decent into Yffiniac, later to be famous as the home of Bernard Hinault. The last stage of the 9 day Tour de L'Ouest in September 1959, came up this road, well known for the Onion sellers, with their products hung out for sale at the side of the road. Tom was able to put this knowledge to good use in this race won by the Breton Job Morvan. Tom won stage 4 into Quimper and stage 5, a time trial, plus two third places on other stages. He went on to finish a magnificent 4th place in the world road race championship at Zandvoort, Holland, behind Andre Darrigade, astounding everyone and cementing a professional contract. When Tom was staying in the Murphy household the previous year, the 2 sons who also raced were living at home, the elder brother was quite good, his progress had been curtailed when he was called up for National Service. It turned out that Monsieur Murphy was a heavy drinker, not surprising working in an abattoir in those days, as they were quite primitive. As I can vouch for, having had the almost compulsory tour, which I prefer to forget. When the Monsieur came home at lunch time, after having had the inevitable aperitive with his workmates, he sat down with the rest of us, with a full bottle of red wine in front of him, which he drank to himself, whilst the rest of us had water.

As there is no racing in Brittany in January, I quickly left to go south.

St Brieuc to Barcelona and Tarragonna

On the route to Barcelona, I stayed mostly at youth hostels; I know which ones as I found my old youth hostel card, perhaps, I kept it thinking I was Peter Pan. This then is the route I took, Nantes, Saint, Villeneuve sur Lot, Caesarean, Toulouse, Beziers Perpignan; all these hostels were excellent. Not stamped on the card was Bordeaux because the place was in a very poor state, there were no other guests, no one in charge either, the outside temperature was freezing in the night, not helped by no glass in the windows. Not surprisingly, I did not linger finding a bar that was open very early for coffee and croissants. The state of the hostel seemed to depend on if the local authority was either left or right wing, obviously this Bordeaux area was on the right. On route, I called to see Tom in the Rapha Gitane training camp in the foothill of the Pyrenees, it being adjacent to the route I was taking. Surprisingly, for such a big team, it was a small very modest hotel; Tom was sharing a cramped room with Brian Robinson, who no doubt was able to add to his education. Tom took me into the bar and bought me a beer I thought he might have treated me to a croque monsieur or something, no not even an introduction to anyone, he could have said another bloody anglaise who thinks he might succeed as a racing cyclist, but Tom was Tom.

On arrival in Barcelona, I managed with great difficulty after two or three days to track down a race organiser in a local bar, after several days of meetings and much animated debate, I could not speak Spanish but could read the animations, which are similar the world over when passions run high. Finally, from a higher authority, perhaps even Franco as it seemed to be a matter of life or death, they obtained for me a special one day's licence, changing the race category to international. The race stared at 11 am slap bang in the middle of Barcelona, an extremely busy city in which it is difficult for an everyday cyclist to thread his way through the streets. It is to be noted that nowadays the locals have endeavoured to solve the problem by riding scooters, which are everywhere almost like a plague of locusts. I wondered how we would fare with the traffic but we need not have worried. Two policemen on motor bikes roared away in front of the bunch, and there was another policia at every crossroad to stop the traffic.

The first five miles or so were over a cobbled highway, then we swung off on to lesser roads that climbed into the mountains. Often, the road virtually disappeared and there was nothing but a track of loose stones or wet slippery clay. Conditions were far worse than any I had ever come across in Belgium, that is saying something. You either had to stay on the bike or become a horrible sticky mess in the middle of the road. To make matters worse, every time we came to a village where we had to do a tour of the back alleys, presumably to give a better view to a mas of wildly cheering spectators. In such conditions, it was not surprising that by the half way mark, about 40 miles, the bunch had been reduced to ten. I was the tenth just hanging on by the skin of my teeth. There were four in front; the rest were struggling behind or had abandoned.

Finally, the string broke on the last col 15 miles from the finish and I was on my own, I never saw them again until the outskirts of Barcelona when I caught them up in the sag waggon. I have an idea a lot of money changed hands on whether I finished or not; apparently, the organisers had gambled on my not finishing as I was invited to join them immediately afterwards for a meal, I can tell you I *was very hungry*. That was it for the time being; no more racing in Spain, so it was back to the youth hostel in Barcelona where I stayed for one month.

The Hostel in Barcelona was something else altogether, nowadays it would be classed as a Parador; today, it probably is that at a different price entirely as I can vouch, having stayed in one on 3 July 2020 on my way home from France after the lock in. Very substantial meals were precisely at 15.00 hours and 21.00 hours with typically Catalan faire accompanied by some very excellent wine. My favourite was identical to the French sauternes you can buy today, if you can afford it. All the wine being drank from the Spanish wine pitcher, the porron, which holds a full bottle of wine. Drinking from these porrons is an art in itself; the utensil does not touch the lips; the wine being poured directly into your mouth. Whilst staying there, I became friendly with a Spaniard also staying in the hostel, called Gomez, he was to explain much about Spain and Barcelona in particular. Most interesting even at that time was the Sagrada Familia Church where construction began in 1883, later taken over by the architectural genius GAUDI who transformed the project to his own style. This was under construction at a very modest pace at the time of my visit. In 1984, UNESCO designated it as a World Heritage Site. It is a source of Spanish pride that work continues to this day; in 2019, the date of my last visit work was continuing at some pace.

Using to the fullest the facilities of the hostel were the Phalangist party who were the sole legal party of General Franco; membership of his party became indispensable to political advancement; they officially had a strong emphasis to the Catholic religious identity. According to Gomez, the large group in the hostel was made up of selected new members, one from each village or town to undergo further training (indoctrination), including the priests among them. Each morning, they were lined up like a military unit in the hostel's substantial quadrangle, where they were marched up and down chanting and singing.

One morning I was requested to go and see the general in charge; having no choice, I went to see him resplendent in military uniform braids medals and all, they thought at that time they had to impress the British. Not surprisingly, he wanted to know why I was there. I explained that I was merely training in a warmer climate on my bike before returning for the racing season in Brittany. Seeming satisfied, they did not bother me anymore. I noticed that Gomez kept a low profile keeping well out of the Philangists way. He was also to show me the seamier side of Barcelona; I was extremely surprised to see that under Franco the Raval, or Upper Ramblas, if you want to find it, assuming it still exists, made Soho and the Pigalle seem tame, from what I gleaned. My friend went on to claim that many of the Philangists, particularly the priests, spent the evening visiting this area, which I did not doubt seeing the state some of them were in the next morning.

On to Tarragona

After this super educative sojourn in Barcelona, my friend said he was travelling on to Tarragona Youth Hostel and would I like to meet him there, so I did. This hostel was almost a duplicate of the previous one set in even lusher grounds that only a Catalan climate can produce in the winter.

Tarragona is a medieval old town with many ancient Roman ruins including a Roman amphitheatre and Chariot track. Again, I had the guided tour one day to see the cathedral. The Sagrada Familia in Barcelona is not a cathedral but a church. Whilst walking down one of the isles, we saw this small round very corpulent priest walking by chance towards us, to my great surprise on reaching us he said, "Oh! Its Gomes. Is it really you?" Then something about his family which I did not follow, "Please both of you, come to my quarters." On reaching his quarters, he had a transistor radio playing very loudly the song Jezebel. The last time I had heard the same song was lying in the sun at the Heights of Abraham, quite appropriately on a club run to Matlock Bath. The song went something like *If ever a pair of eyes promised paradise it was you zezebel it was you zezebel.*

Judging by the sumptuous quarter of our priest, obviously he was more than a priest, one would assume he was already in paradise. His furnishing and paintings would elegantly fit into any stately home plus a view through the window of an inner courtyard with a fountain and small garden that would do justice to the Alhambra. At one end of the room was a substantial floor to ceiling cupboard at one side of which was a much smaller floor to ceiling alter. Our host proceeded to open the cupboard saying, "Will you join me in a cognac?" which of course we did. After this he said, "We have a special liquor only brewed for us at the Monastery of Monserrat, we will try that next."

My impression was that Gomez was the descendent of a wealthy Spanish family forced out of Spain by the civil war. Gomez had nothing to say as to this; after our further month's sojourn Gomez announced he was going to Mallorca, would I like to come. I was in two minds, but declined setting of back to Saint Brieuc, not knowing at that time that I had a destiny to come in Mallorca.

I returned by a route similar to my arrival staying in many of the same hostels, of course, giving the one at Bordeaux a wide berth. Notedly, the villages in the countryside before I left Spain were rather impoverished and neglected with many women dressed very soberly working in the fields. Very much in contrast to the luxury that our host had in Tarragona Cathedral. One of many highlights of my return was a visit to the medieval Citadel of Carcassonne with its numerous watchtowers incorporated in its doubled walled fortifications, further fortified with deep moats. At that time, the road passed in front of the fortifications; nowadays, you do not have the same view but substantial renovations have been carried out. Nowadays, Carcassonne is very popular with tourists and well worth a visit.

Following Tom Simpson to St Brieuc 1960

On return, I had a new co-lodger who I had not known of previously. Sean Ryan who hailed from Rawmarsh three miles from my home. Together, we were introduced to Tom's previous club: Club Olympic Briochin, COB for short; they had facilities in the local sports hall, what we would now call a multi-sports complex, although it was not up to that standard. The COB was not just for cyclists but other sports as well; the man in charge, in this case, the trainer had made his name on the phenomenal success of Tom the previous year; he continued to enjoy this accolade for the rest of his career at the COB. I personally cannot see what he contributed as a trainer to cycling disciplines, although to be fair as the club membership was large and diverse perhaps, he deserved this reputation with his contribution to other sports. Among the riders at the club was a young Dany Le Bert, the son of Robert Le Bert, the famous soigneur of Louison Bobet. I became friendly with Dany; also I became friendly with riders from the three other clubs in Saint Brieuc.

My racing in March started slowly to begin with until I adjusted to the racing speed. My first success was at the Grand Prix Des Espoir's at the village of Henahiban a modest third and fourth category event which included first and second year juniors from age 16. To start with, I was given a third category licence; it did not matter that I was a first cat in the UK. Tom himself was issued with a fourth cat licence, but they were not going to let that happen again. The circuit unusually reminded me of racing in Belgium; I had previously spent a short holiday at the Café Den Engels in Gent, the domain of Albert Burick; I will talk about that later. Suffice to say, the roads were wet gravelly twisty and narrow; I soon found the safest place was at the front. No doubt assisted by my ride to Spain, I had the racing form, so I was away alone in front, cheered on by a good crowd the cry of encouragement at this time was *allez allez Robic*. This cry became familiar for the rest of year, not often enough in my direction.

I rode with Robic in the years 1960-61; he was still riding at 40, quite old for that era; he won the Tour de France in 1947, his nickname was Biquet. Even the less important races had very good crowds; in those days, nobody had cars so they had nowhere else to go. The bigger professional races held in bigger towns attracted enormous crowds, approaching football crowds, people found a way to get there from surrounding villages. This was a very good start as being out alone in front meant that I collected a good collection of primes, which were payable in cash on the day which was very useful.

The primes were the responsibility of the commentator (speaker). A good speaker was a tremendous asset; he was good at entertaining the crowd, knowing all about the riders, he was able to impart much knowledge, all part of the task in obtaining more cash from everyone; of course, he had a well-deserved percentage. Probably the best speaker at the time was Mario Cotti of Argentinian decent; he was the speaker at the Tour de France before Daniel Mangeas, part of his chatter was he would always tell you who was last in the peloton, probably me. It was very disconcerting; for example, when you were flat out passing the finishing line, I do mean flat out to hear "Francis Le Behan deux minutes en tete," two minutes in front on his own. You were not alone thinking that it was impossible, how can he do that. Suffice to say he died of a heart attack at an early age, after retirement.

The prize money went down to the 15th place more for the bigger races; this was paid in cash to the federation; in this case, the Committee de Bretagne. This was paid to your club for distribution at the year end, sometimes interim payments were made. All the money came from the organisers efforts in obtaining donations and sponsorship from all and sundry, local and national businesses, individuals; even the local and regional authorities played their part. I managed to stay another month with the Murphy family, that was it, Robert the youngest son was pleasant enough, I never met the older brother, but the bottle of wine being consumed by one person together with the long face was enough, so I moved out; Sean staying. Pleasingly, I found boarding and lodging at a reasonable price in a small residential residence on Boulevard Charner, near the railway station which was convenient this first year. Later, for a time, I had another cycling co-resident, Jim Moor from Manchester he was a handy rider but I believe he had trouble making enough money to pay his bills. I did not see him the following year, he had given it a good go, later making his reputation as a 6-day rider in the first London 6 day.

Later, when I saw Tom at one of the races, I asked him how he had put up with the father. He said, "It was not so bad when the two sons were at home," as they travelled together to races, even so he wished he had obtained the courage to find somewhere else.

Most people think of Brittany as flat, especially when commentators and journalists talk of the flat Brittany stages in the Tour De France, nothing could be further from the truth. In between St Brieuc and Paimpol are the highest cliffs in Brittany; consequently, when the road drops down to the sea in the valleys, they can be quite long, even steep in places. As the riders found out in the 1995 T De F stage of Dinan to Lannion when they climbed the 20% gradient out of the Port de Brehec. St Brieuc is not for nothing known as the City of the Valleys. Inland, there are some good climbs where the landscape can be similar to Peak District in places, Mur de Bretagne is well noted as is the Monts D Arree in the triangle between Huelgoat, Guerlesquin and Chateaulin. Especially do not forget the numerous enchanting mythical forests such as the forest de Paimpont which are simply magical to ride through, changing with the seasons. Travelling in those days was very pleasant with very little traffic, you could ride inland among a myriad of small roads with a view of the sea. In the villages, almost all the women were dressed in black, on the farms, you saw only horses no tractors at all. I trained sometimes with Sean Ryan or Ron Coe mostly alone you did not need to do an enormous mileage once the season was in full swing as we could race three times a week, sometimes more.

Father and Father's Trip to France

Later, when Monsieur Aubrey, the proprietor of my residence had told everyone that my father was coming from the UK to see what I was up to, a reception was arranged for the evening in the restaurant where I ate most days. I did not suspect I had many fans, but rather that they wanted to meet the man who was riding all the way from South Yorkshire, to them a distant place, who was obviously more of a rider than the son.

Before I relate what was an epic journey, it will help if first, I tell you more about my father. He was born Norman Joshua Neale, the Joshua being after his father's name, presumably why he was known as Josh, he was quite a character. The story in his family, he had eight brothers and sisters, is that as a young child along with a friend, they became bored with the pontification at the local chapel on Sunday. *Who would not be?* Going outside, they saw the key in the lock and locked the door, subsequently losing the key. Understandably, he never went to chapel again, as he was banned. Did I tell you he was also intelligent? Josh was secretary of my first cycling club-the Mexborough Road Club, not to be confused with the obviously less successful Mexborough Wheelers, who could boast a certain Bill

Cheadle as a member, before we snaffled him in our club, I think the attraction was called Betty.

My father presumably became secretary in 1939 when all the male members left to go to war, never to return, holding this position until the club became defunct in the 1980s. He was an iron moulder by trade, very hard physical work which was a reserved occupation during the war. My father had a passion for horse racing and to a limited extent, the gambling that went with it, this was his only means of transport as it was for everyone at this time. This was how he meet my mother Clarice, herself from a family of eight; they rode tandem together up to the day they were married, then she never rode again. It being normal that at the weekend, the father had to look after the son, so I rode on a cushion on my father's crossbar to all the local race meetings, Doncaster, Pontefract Wetherby, York etc. My father who was small lightweight was often mistaken for a jockey and asked for tips. He missed his way; it would have been easier as well as more profitable being a tipster instead of an iron moulder.

On writing to my parents, I explained to my father that if he wanted, he could easily come to St Brieuc by riding to Southampton, catching the ferry to St Malo, then crossing the Rance by local ferry to Dinard. This he could do in his summer holidays; it being an easy ride for him along the coast to St Brieuc. The big day arrived, the reception committee eagerly awaiting his arrival in the evening, at the bar. The evening wore on, no father yet, more beer, still no father, more beer, it was getting dark, no father still more beer, it became dark no father. Despite all the beer, everyone had become rather anxious. "Oh! You should ring the Hospital Police Pompiers etc." I was the only one quite calm assuring everyone that he would arrive, he did quite late in the dark with no lights, more beer.

Eventually, some days later, I obtained the full story of why he was so late, he failed to take the ferry across the Rance arriving in Dinan thinking it was Dinard; at that time, the tidal power station had not been built, there being no bridge across the Rance. Being rather lost, he managed to find a local priest who had spent some time in Ireland and spoke English. He explained to my father to take the other river bank to Dinard which obviously had increased his distance. Finally, arriving in Dinard, he then took the coast road towards St Brieuc. Thinking he had arrived in St Brieuc, he could not find Boulevard Charner, which I had explained was next to the railway station. Of course, he could not as he was in the beautiful coastal resort of St Briac. Setting off again you can imagine he was now becoming rather hungry; he had a few francs in the local currency, left over from a previous trip to Paris, that I never learned a word about. So, he called in the local 'epicerie' grocers' shop to see what he could obtain with the few francs he had. He bought a bottle of wine, as he did not have enough money to buy any food. The chocolate he was bringing me, as it hardly existed in Western France at that time, became consumed along with the wine.

Naturally, after this, he was tired, being the middle of summer, he was soon fast asleep, oblivious of the fact that there were probably adders in the grass. Suitably refreshed, he set off again but after sometime, he was uneasy; something was wrong, finally, he realised the sea was on the left not the right, turning round, he finally arrived at his destination the same day even though it was almost midnight.

1960 Continued
Racing in St Brieuc

Occasionally, races were close enough to St Brieuc to ride to the start; often, I had a lift with Andre Ruffet who was grateful for a contribution towards the petrol. Otherwise, I was able to travel by bus or train on the local branch lines, in the red and white diesels. With the bus, your bike was often strapped on the front, which looked rather bizarre. There was a good local rail network in those days; some of these lines still exist, Paimpol-Guingamp among others for example, the splendid route follows the river estuary of the Trieux from Paimpol to Pontrieux. There is a tourist steam train in the season which I can highly recommend. As races usually stared at 3 pm, this made travel easy; there were also some evening criteriums and track meetings, mostly nocturns. Sometimes, I would stay overnight in a youth hostel, my favourite was at Guerlescan which was as good as a 3-star hotel to me. I used this hostel frequently for the next three years even when I had a car.

Very often, many riders from different areas depending on where the race was, congregated to a particular restaurant, often it was the one at Gourin. A special meal suitable for racing cyclists, at a special price was prepared; usually it consisted of a tomatoes and ham starter, steak or fish main course, yoghurt desert. Always the restaurant was lively humming with a tremendous camaraderie rarely experienced anywhere else, what pleased me no Georges Grousard or Job Morvan in sight.

The evening nocturns were mostly on very tight technical circuits calling for a high degree of skill and nerve, these types of races could be up to 50 laps, hence many primes, the afternoon races 15-25 laps. Your skills were called into question the more laps there were as even a yard lost on a corner eventually took its toll, unless you were superman. The afternoon circuit races had their advantages as you did not have to know the circuit, but this helped, you could get the feel of the race after a few laps. No races were less than 100 km except the evening nocturnes, the rest much longer and faster than the circuit races in the UK. Of course, with any racing it paid to know the opposition. The problem with anything involving money is things become complicated in so far as different alliances are formed to try to divide the prize money to the advantage of the riders in the alliance, otherwise known as the Mafia.

The Mafia changed dependent on the terrain of the circuit, some were much hillier than others; some faster, some extremely hard, the finishes also varied. Certain of the most important races commanded starting money, this varied according to the standing of the rider stars like Anquetil could receive the equivalent of 300 euros or more, Tom 150-200 euros, the local stars Le Bihan, Bourles, Ruffet, Le Borgne, Simon, Le Bigault, Le Buhotel, Cloarec, less, me 40 euros at best, nothing the first year. Of course, there were primes and a general classification in addition. The stars were mostly interested in primes or the kudos in winning, they sometimes brought team mates who rode for them; mostly one assumed the team mates were given free rein for additional money as unless they were very well known, they were unlikely to receive starting money. Part of the game was to show the talent of the Bretagne's who were often better than many of the stars in this type of race. Many had ridden the classics or Tour de France as domestics in teams, but it did not take them long to realise they could have an easier life by riding the Brittany criteriums and in many cases, earn more this way.

There were a limited number of shorter stage races, mostly based at one location to keep costs down, often promoted by the local newspaper or food and drink suppliers. Once a week you saw your club secretary to choose and enter the races you were going to ride. This had to be one week in advance; there being no entry on the line as in Belgium.

Many of the towns and villages where we raced, Breton was the predominant language that we heard. Celtic Breton, a Celtic language was spoken to the west of St Brieuc in the triangle with Lannion to the west, Rostrenen to the south. My own village Plouha where I now live is right on the border to the east; three or four years ago, the French-only road signs in my village were replaced by dual signs even though nobody here now speaks Breton. Central Brittany towards Quimper Gallo Breton, a Romance language is spoken. With the passage of time, the Breton language areas have diminished. During both world wars, particularly the first, the Breton troop could only speak Breton, consequently the Paris military command abused the Breton troops very badly. This must go some way to explaining why for some Britons, Parisians are not their favourite people. Whilst to the east of St Brieuc, they spoke only French.

Sean Ryan and I rode a few races in the villages towards Dinard. One of the riders we frequently were to encounter was a young Georges Grousard, he was one year older than myself; he hailed from Fougeres always coming with several helpers, no doubt due to the influence of his successful brother Joseph who had some big wins including the Milan San Remo, to his name. Georges created an impressive image; he was not very big, with powerful looking big legs, being the only rider being seen to have a massage before the race. It seemed to become a regular pattern in these races that Sean and myself finished fourth or fifth in different orders with Georges just one place behind us, but we must not forget that somehow Georges won one of these races; we must have been asleep. This must have rankled with him or perhaps he was just unsociable as he never bothered to speak to us not even a bonjour. Later, when Georges career ended after riding in seven Tour de Frances, holding the yellow jersey for seven consecutive days in 1964; he made a living in his hometown of Fougeres as a buraliste (selling cigarettes); he organised many of the local races; in this area, when I raced there as veteran, probably to supplement his income.

No doubt, he must have known me, everybody else did, but I never ever had a smile or a bonjour. One other rider back in the 60s that I never received a bonjour from was Job Morvan; perhaps he was one of only a few who spoke Breton or wanted to speak only Breton. Otherwise, these two were an absolute exception, as to everyone else their comportment was unblemished, apart from the English visitors urinating in the flowers. I cannot say that is the case in other walks of life, especially where money is involved.

In this year, I saw Tom about three times in Brittany where he had a contract to race; we went round to various places to recover items of equipment he had stashed away.

One time he had the loan of one of the iconic future looking Citroens with the innovative hydraulic suspension with a view to buying it trying it out on some very rough gravelly roads at great speed, I thought it was fabulous, I had never experienced anything like it. It was a surprise when he did not buy it, I think he bought a Panhard in the end. At this time, he told me his story of how he came to meet a certain young lady having heard that there was a young English girl working as an au pair in the town, he had the address and set off to meet her. He set off to find the address and became evermore frustrated in his attempts; I suppose also the language was a barrier; his attempts at politeness finally failed him; his language rather deteriorated finally he swore very badly when saying something like I suppose you don't know where this! *!*!*! address is. It turned out this was Helen, who he eventually married; she came from Norton Doncaster not far from where Tom had lived. Much later, when I met Helen, when she was married by now to Barry Hoban, I did not think it prudent to raise any questions.

Surprisingly, I never learned any language at school even though I had gained a scholarship studying commercial subjects for three years, it has been a mystery ever since those languages were absent from the curriculum. When I arrived in St Brieuc, I knew only oui and non, however you soon learn the numbers and money, it is essential to know what the announcer is saying in races as to the primes etc., if you don't learn, you won't eat; it's that simple. Another important thing was to be able to argue with the finishing judges, there were no photo finishes in those days. Like everybody else, you had to claim a position one or two places better in order to receive the real one; it was also the case that these officials had made a good contribution to the decline of the beer stocks. Consequently, I learned my French bit by bit, by learning some words and putting some together you arrive eventually. My command and understanding are very good, my grammar is not always correct; my friends say I have a special version of Franglaise, but they understand me perfectly.

Of course, food is a great motivation to learn a language. Brittany is particularly noted for its sea food, one crustacean in particular coquille Saint-Jacques (clams) is mostly dragged for the seabed in the Bay of St Brieuc. Also, mussels, oysters and lobster are retrieved along most of the coast, one had a good view of the oyster and mussel beds when riding the splendidly rugged and jagged coastline, among the best views were between Yffiniac and Val-Andre also towards Paimpol my favourite was one of the many back roads around Port Lazo. Other noted specialities were Crepes and Gallets, most of the restaurants were there to serve the locals at lunch time with their Menu Ouvrier (workers menu). There were not the plethora of fast-food restaurants that you see today; certainly, no McDonalds, Mc Do's as they are known to the French. Along the coast in the tourist spots, Plateau Armorican, crab, lobster, oysters, crevettes, crayfish, mussels, se snails all artistically piled up on a big dish in the centre of the table, you do not see it very often now only in the most expensive restaurants.

One day I sat on my own in a small inland restaurant when a British tourist came in with his young son; they proceeded to order a bottle of wine with their meal, they ignored me thinking I was a local, so I sat dumbo. When the bottle came, he had trouble pouring the wine as there was a large piece of branch or root in the bottle, something I have never seen before or since, *does the wine always come like that, the youngster said, yes said the father it gives it flavour.* I don't know how I kept my face straight, wisely, I kept my mouth shut.

Wine is of course very important to the French, the nearest wine area to Brittany is the Loire; from there, the wine that is mostly drunk with the fish courses is Muscadet and Gross Plant white wine varieties, many wine writers seem to regard the Gross Plant variety as cheaper, thus being inferior to the Muscadet, I can tell them that most Bretons think otherwise. Wine is rarely a prize in the criteriums, in one particular criterium, I was surprised to find I had won rather a good selection of wines as primes; I had no idea how good or bad they were; on my next midday meal, I showed the wines to the proprietor Mr Aubrey; he was impressed with these wines, so we did a swap for my normal red wine, the extra bottles I gained lasted well into the following year, thus keeping my bills down.

On an evening very often, I would meet with friends, Georges Le Lart, Pierre Hamon, Georges Le Pennec, Dany Le Bert in a bar in the town centre ran by Georges Le Bouris and his wife. Most of us drank Cabernet de Anjou which is a sweet rosy wine from the Loire, not to my taste now, or any of the others for that matter. Apart from other pastimes, such as visiting the markets, which I still do, they are part of normal life. Swimming was indulged in which to a very limited extent, including laying on the beach, sheltered from the sun. It seemed to me that despite climate change, it was warmer at that time, apart from admiring the local talent which was all one could do, because their fathers kept them locked up at night, well most of them. A little swim did no harm as to your racing, contrary to Beryl Burton, who at this time thought cold water on the legs was a complete anathema, she even sat in the shower on a stool with her legs completely out of the shower so that they would not get wet.

In the middle of the season, I started to have cramps in the legs without any reason; even riding a few kilometres. Being due to ride a 3-day race in a few days' time, I rested completely thinking I would be ok after in the race; this was not the case, after a few kilometres, I had to climb off. Immediately, Dany Le Bert arranged for me to see his father who had a physiotherapy practice in town; he was the famous soigneur to Louison Bobet, so there was no one with a higher reputation. Giving me a good examination, he said, "Nice pair of legs. Normally it is only women that say that," adding, "I can see no reason at all for your cramps. I can do nothing." Fortunately, after about a week or so, I was back to normal and recovered. It was many years later when I was in my forties that the same thing happened again when I was racing for my club at Quintin. Fortunately, I was referred to the club's sports doctor; he demanded if I had been eating shellfish, the answer to which was in the affirmative. "Ah!" he said, "its food poisoning." After a few days on antibiotics, I was alright, mystery solved.

We were at the end of the season; it has always struck me as rather stupid to start the season early when the weather is least agreeable yet finish early when there is plenty of good weather left. Still there was one big event remaining the wedding of our friend, fellow rider Pierre Hamon. This being my first French wedding, I did not know what to expect. George Le Lart said, "We will pick you up Friday"; to which I replied, "The wedding is not until Saturday."

So, George said with a grin, "We are starting Friday afternoon."This then was the start of a grand tour of the friends and relatives who lived God only knows where in the countryside that I doubt even the occupying Germans failed to discover. This was an extremely hospitable mystery tour; I refused the hooch (eau de vie in this part of the world a derivative of cider), neither did I like the idea of mixing wine with cider especially the heaver homemade variety, so I stuck to the red wine eating something at the same time where possible. I have vague recollection of various boites de nuit (discos) in the night although I did not know they even existed at the time.

Saturday, the wedding went well; I thought our little band were well behaved if looking slightly the worst for wear. Afterwards, the visits continued all of Saturday night till the morning when I was told, "Right, we have to see they have the soup."

"What soup?" I said.

"Oh! It's the tradition that the young marrieds have the soup de noce, (honeymoon soup)." In the early misty hours in what Wordsworth would describe as the season of mists and mellow fruitfulness which applied equally to what was then called the Cotes de Nord. Then missed. As to Woodsworth's beloved Lake District, going not very far, the couple was sensibly being careful with the costs, we went and disturbed them from their bed, watching to make sure they drank the soup. That was the end of the drinking for me or almost because I went to epicerie, buying several bottles of milk which I will say went down very well. After the celebrations, George had announced that he would be leaving to live and work in Montreal. I was sorry as it appeared; I was likely to lose a friend, this proved not to be the case even though the move was definitive. I will write more about this later. Postscript (The Cotes du Nord underwent a change of name to the Cotes D'Amor because it was thought the original name gave a cold image deterring tourism).

London 1960/61 and UK Before 1960

At the end of the season, I returned to the UK staying with an aunty in East Finchley, London for several weeks and not riding the bike very much, doing more sightseeing as it was all new to me. Profiting from this stay, I met Jock Wadley the editor of the *Sporting Cyclist*, a monthly magazine, meeting him in his club over a meal and a bottle of red wine. Of course, cyclists drink the red not the white as this can give them cramps. He ordered it by the name claret, I only thought of this when I looked up the articles I had written for him, as over the years I have been in the habit of calling at Pugnac a wine cooperative near Bordeaux to pick up a few bottles. These last two or three years, they have started selling a wine and labelling it Claret, while it is a Bordeaux, it is not a wine that would have been called a claret in the past; this one is half way between a red and a rosy, I recommend that you try it.

As a Youngster

I remember Reg Harris racing against the Dutch champion Arie Van Vliet on the cinder track at the local Brodsworth Miners Gala. They must have had the money to pay these two, before Arthur Scargill got his hands on it. Yes, it was a big thrill to me and the locals, even though I eventually worked out how this double act worked. Reg won in the UK, Arie in Holland. In Doncaster, we had an even bigger act than these two, none other than local cyclist Dereck Atter, known to all and sundry as the MAD HATTER. At this time, he worked at the Doncaster Railway workshops, known as Doncaster Plant which employed about 3,000 or 4,000 people. This industry along with mining and steel making was the predominant work where I was born and lived. My connection with Doncaster Plant is that on the 3 July 1938, a steam locomotive, the Mallard built at this plant, broke the world steam locomotive record at 126 mph, which still stands to this day. I arrived in the world on the 5 July, perhaps early with the excitement or late with the suspense. None of the stories I will relate about Dereck are made up; you just could not make them up. I believe they symbolise the humour of the area.

Dereck was a keen racer; his prowess being noted by many at the plant works. Apparently, two younger workers were not impressed for some reason that Dereck was any good, telling him so. Dereck rather rashly made it clear that he could beat them with one leg, not unsurprisingly, this was ridiculed. Being the deep thinker that Dereck undoubtedly was, he thought very carefully about this, before coming to a plan of action. Afterwards, the Hatter mind worked as only it can, coming to a plan, he challenged them to a race for money with him using only one leg, conditional that he chose where and when the race was to be held, they both had to beat him. He reasoned that as they only rode to work, they would have no stamina, therefore deciding that the race would be to Whitby, over the Yorkshire Wolds. Of course, Dereck had already experimented with riding over the hills with one leg, So, the competition was arranged, all the plant learned of the forthcoming event. As you would imagine in a works of this magnitude, an enormous amount of money was placed in this bet. There was only one outcome, Dereck of course was the victor; I never learned what he did with the money, probably he saved it to buy the pet shop he owned much later.

Two Touring Trips

were made to the continent before I went to St Brieuc in 1960, the first with two friends Dave and Graham, riding first to Dover, then taking the ferry across to Ostend, the flat countryside making for easier riding than in our native Yorkshire. Otherwise, Belgium to us was not a lot different to the UK, including the plentiful supply of fish and chips. Although in Belgium unlike the UK, mussels and chips were a staple meal readily available. First leg being to Bruges as many have done before us, then Gent, which was later to become more familiar to me. Then on to Brussels where we had the superb and unique experience of visiting the 1958 Brussels World Fair, the first World Expo after WW 2 which showcased the best technological advancements of the time. What stood out expressly to us was the Atomium which weighed in at 2,400 tons, representing a magnetised crystal cell. This is still there to this day, becoming an iconic landmark on the Brussels skyline.

After this, on to Luxemburg where the terrain was a little more to our liking. Which was later confirmed by my riding the veterans Tour of Luxemburg 5-day race, seven times. Afterwards back to Ostend, arriving very hungry almost penniless and struggling to scrape enough money together to buy something to eat. Dave and Graham put their money together buying fish and chips; I just had enough to buy a loaf of bread, then selling half of this to them receiving the remainder of their money, which bought me fish and chips, not a bad deal.

The following year, I became more ambitious doing a similar thing with a friend Lauri Rissbrook. From Belgium, it was on to Bastogne in the Ardennes, keeping an eye open to see if there were any remnants of the Panzer corps still lurking after the Ardennes offensive of 1944, then on to Luxemburg. From here to Switzerland, vising such places as Lake Lucerne, Interlaken plus many other breathtakingly scenic places. Of course, all the different countries that we passed through had different currencies, Belgium, Luxemburg, Germany, France, before arriving in Switzerland. Laurie found the different currencies even more frustrating than I did, trying to pay forever in the wrong currency. As we were only poor Schmucks not having much in the way of notes, but a lot of coinage which weighed us down on the Swiss Mountains. Switzerland, not having the astronomical prices of today, we booked a room in a small square with a fountain.

Laurie said if I pay in the wrong coinage again, it's all going in that fountain, inevitable it did; in anger, the entire coinage went in. **Another advantage we now have in Europe is mostly a single currency.** Waking up in the middle of the night, I saw Laurie's bed was empty, looking out the window much to my amusement, but not surprise, there he was fishing his money back out of the fountain. Our route took us back through France, where I developed terrible toothache, suffering pain as well as being half wheeled to boot. On arrival at our next overnight stop, our host fixed me up with a dental appointment. On entering the dentist's premises, what a dismal place it turned out to be, probably in an earlier life a Gestapo torture chamber. Very soberly dressed older people crowded the waiting room, who all moved out of the way when I arrived, even the guy in the dentist's chair was kicked out of the room or so it seemed to me. "Ha," the quack said after the examination, "you have a very nasty double tooth at the back which will have to come out, no problem to an expert like me." At least that is what I thought he said as I could not speak French at the time, he could not speak English. After a gigantic struggle with the tooth breaking off, I knew we were finished when he made gestures for me to pay him; probably, I was the only client who paid him. The pain did not end there, I was on pain killers for the rest of the journey; on returning home I discovered he had left the roots in. This was a one-off experience as far a French dentists were concerned.

I have nothing but the highest praise for them, I would say that wouldn't I, one of my best friends for the last 20 years, Loic is now retired from that profession. After the dentist, the half wheeling continued until we found a very reasonably priced little restaurant in Paris which I have since learned would have been a worker's restaurant with a 'Menu Ouvrier.' Drinks and everything was included at a set price, there was a carafe of red wine on the table, which of course we had to try. Laurie could not drink it, saying, "It tasted like vinegar"; it being the first time either of us had drank French wine. Coming out of the restaurant, I was on top of the world, Laurie did not look very happy, especially as it was me now doing the half wheeling. Thus, began my love affair with wine, particularly French Reds, later to extend to a wider choice. Arriving at Ostend, we had made sure we had enough money to buy fish and chips, although if Laurie had not fished his money out of the fountain, this is not certain.

Club Life Before 1960

After the adventures on the cushion of my dad's bike to the races, my first club run of any distance was to Edwinstowe at the age of 15. After a snack stop, in somebody's now-famous tea rooms, we had a very short stroll to the Major Oak, Robin Hoods tree in Sherwood Forest, then just a tree. In the years 1953-59 which I am talking about, we had the pleasure of riding to places like Dovedale, in the Peak District, Gunthorpe Bridge, Newark in Nottinghamshire, Otley, Knaresborough in West Yorkshire, even Cleethorpes, this was the golden age of cycle touring. These places are a nightmare to reach now on a bike; it can still be done with difficulty on the back roads. In the winter, no long runs, places like Owston Ferry, Laneham Ferry etc., very rural away from the town culture, where I was tolerated, sat discreetly behind the door in the bar as a 15-year-old.

Not surprisingly, at a young age, I developed a taste for Barley wine; this beer was brewed by most of the local breweries under different labels of which there were many at that time. Our favourite was Donovans from the workshop brewery. They all had one thing in common; they were quite strong, by the time you had ridden home, you were as sober as a judge, not that I was ever any other. Almost always we had an afternoon tea stop at Blythe on the way home, no matter where we had been. This was the Northern Mecca for cycling where I first meet Tom. There were two main cafes, one is known as the ranch, which catered mostly for time trialists, who often stayed the night as the trials were at some unearthly hour in the morning. We normally went to the other one, the posher one, so we thought, the Bungalow.

Sometimes, on a Saturday if there was an important track meeting at Fallowfield, Manchester, a small band of enthusiasts would ride over the Pennines and back to watch. I should add that in going into the Peak District, the most used route was through Sheffield. The tram lines were a nightmare, especially when it rained. Those stupid capes that we had draped over the handlebars, which did not keep your feet dry, did nothing to help, falling off was all too common. Cyclists especially breathed a sigh of relief when the trams were done away with; I was going to say confined to history, but that was not the case; some years later, a modern system was introduced, this was even worse, cars lost control on them. John Tanner had a nasty accident with a car one year, finishing in hospital.

A member of my first club was Bill Cheadle who was to become a lifelong friend, as he later told me doping was not the only form of cheating. There was another way in the local track meetings. Bill claimed he had seen the father of one young rider, when he thought no one was looking, move the handicap marker applicable to his son forward, giving him more start than he was entitled to.

I started racing on the track at the age of 16 years; I never raced on the road until I was 18, I rode a few time trials, they were not my cup of tea. At the season's end, like many, I rode a few hill climbs, Monsul Dale, Brook house, as I remember the only time, I had any sort of result was up the brutish Winnetts Pass. Albert Thorpe (his wife insisted that we call him by his christened name John) who I admired, usually won, among others the Brook house climb; one year, he was beaten by a rider from my hometown Tut Turton, a fluke in my mind. As it was the year end, we all got drunk in the pub afterwards, barley wine being very popular as well as the pints, it should be noted at that time, you were able to buy mild as well as bitter.

Track racing was in fashion during this period with grass and cinder tracks just about everywhere; they were usually held in conjunction with a village carnival or miners gala. Prizes were silverware, cutlery, glassware etc., if you won something you had no need of you, either gave it away or sold it. Harworth Miners Gala is where in the 5-mile scratch, I lapped the field to win the race, surprising among other the well-known track specialist Roy Swinnerton; Tom was not there, unless he was watching. I much preferred the distance races, Devils, Point to Point, etc. I was certainly not a track sprinter, but I did well in the handicap races. At the time, I had a Blue Rotrax frame which was too big for me, but it did the job. I was small lightweight, it helped on the grass track if you were heavier to keep your bike down on the corners. Many riders like me rode to the meetings on their track bike, which of course had a single fixed gear with a pair of racing wheels strapped by means of a bracket to the front wheel. Cane racing wheels were often used, being pretty flexible on what was often uneven grass tracks. In addition, we had a saddle bag full of tools to take the one front brake off as well as to change the gear ratio with the spare sprockets you carried, if necessary. All my life, I have ridden with my front brake on the right, it is a legacy of when I first cycled, we had only one brake on the right.

Mid-week, we had a track race league held one week at a grass track, the following week at a red shale track, the two grass tracks were Goldthorpe and Thurcroft, the shale tracks Brodsworth and Askern. Notables from my first club the, Mexborough Road Club were Albert Thorpe, Graham Lilley and George Place all quite a bit older than me, all much faster, I experience their superiority first hand in 1954 on just reaching my 16th birthday, when in the divisional team pursuit championship, they were one man short, having no choice but to ask me to make the team up, as there were four to count; I am pleased to say I survived and have a third placed championship medal to prove it.

Other riders of note locally on the track were Harry Tompkins who survived national service in the Korean War, Mike Holmes, Mike Bird, Dave Stables all from the Dearne Wheelers, Pete Andrews, Arthur Maxfield, Ike Delbridge, all three with experience going back several years. It was a very keenly fought competitive league; I would say that wouldn't I as I had the most points over the year the last year, I rode in 1959. Occasionally, we rode the league at Nottingham, more often the league on the banked concrete track at Fallowfield, Manchester. It was on one of these evenings that I crashed down the banking, gathering a fair amount of concrete in my left elbow, finishing up in Manchester Royal Infirmary. While laid on the operating table, I could look up into the light and see the surgeon picking pieces of concrete out of my elbow; what was more concerning was I could hear Mick Bird in the waiting room saying to my other two friends Laurie Rissbrook and Dave Stables, "We had better leave him as I am on the early shift at Goldthorpe colliery tomorrow morning." Laurie was a joiner at the Pit, later leaving to become a joinery teacher, Dave also worked at the Pit, later running his own central heating contractor business. Returning home, I had to see the doctor; unfortunately, this resulted in a double dose of penicillin; the resulting penicillin poisoning being far worse than the effects of any crashes I have had.

A feature of the Fallowfield track meeting was that athletes had their own events, among whom was the 4-minute man Steve Banister; as far as I knew the two groups kept entirely apart. If sportspeople cannot interact, what chance have different religions?

Second Year in France 1961

In 1960, among my group of friends was Andre LeGuilliou, Dede to his friends, he was madly supportive of cycling, although he did not ride himself. Despite being an official of another club, he found me a family to stay with across the road from where he lived. This was the family Bienvenu who had five children, the youngest being six months, the oldest 13. They were to become my adopted family, to this day my only family, apart from my new second wife, who was also alone until I met her. Pierre, the father of the family I soon got to know very well, worked on the steam locomotives at the large nearby Engine Works. It transpired as a youngster leaving school at a very early age, he had a job at the St Brieuc port of Le League.

During the war, some of these workers were conscripted as forced labourers being sent to Germany. Pierre being very young was lucky enough to be tipped off by the boss, each time this was to happen, going to hide with his grandparents in the forest at Pontivy. It does not take much imagination to guess what his feelings were towards the Germans. Many years later, the very well-educated grandson came with a young German he had befriended to visit the granddad. Someone asked the question never to be asked, "What did your granddad do in the war?" The immediate answer being, "My grandad was in the Red Cross." The wink that Pierre gave me said it all.

Not only did I have new lodgings but a new club-the Velo Club de Quintin, Quintin being a fortified village 15 kilometres from St Brieuc. Quintin is a medieval walled town on a lake, one-time centre of the weaving industry. Both Ron Coe and I became licenced to this club, who were sponsored by a local drinks company; Limonade Le Menir was the inscription on our racing jerseys. We had entry fees paid with a bonus of so much a kilometre if we won, the only way it would have paid anything worthwhile was if we won an imaginary Tour De Monde. Included in my sponsorship was a racing bike; Ron did not need one as along with John Geddes, Bertin Cycles provided them with their bikes.

Our first big race in 1961 was the Tour De Loire and Chere, in a British team that included Michael Wright. Later, among his many wins were three stages of the Tour De France. Michael grew up living in Liege, Belgium, the Walloon area, where they spoke French. His father had died in WW2, his mother had remarried a Belgium soldier, Michael, benefited from dual nationality, but did not speak English at all. Ron and I travelled direct to the race before returning to Brittany after the race. From Yorkshire, we travelled down the new M1 motorway in Ron's van, being my first time on the M1. My impression was that it was downhill all the way. A gleaming new comet aircraft was waiting to take us the short flight to Blois, where the race started. In a race where the weather was hot and humid, the only result of note was Ron narrowly being beaten into second place in the last days bunch finish, he went on to register three wins in this year, retiring in the Tour de France after stage 5.

Back racing in Brittany where all too often we had a minuets silence, at the start of a race for a local or some young rider who had been conscripted for National Service and losing his life in the Algerian War. This war ended on 19 March 1962 with that country's independence. Often locals came to talk to me in English, which was often better than my French, recounting their experience of WW2 and where they had been in the UK, usually Plymouth, Portsmouth, Liverpool, London. If you are interested in learning more of the local war time history, a good place to start is the Museum De La Resistance at St Connan, Cote D'Armor, this honours the memory of the patriots fighting to liberate themselves from the Nazis. The museum is pleasantly set on a lake with a very nice restaurant; that based on my last visit, I do not hesitate in recommending.

One very amusing instance occurred at the start of one local race that I cannot comprehend to this day. Two very young native Africans appeared on the start line, they were very black, very tall, most likely on this description from Chad. They were immaculately dressed in white racing jerseys and brand-new bikes; everybody was in awe, when the mayor cut the tape for the start, they disappeared to everybody's amazement up the road at great speed; after about 4 kilometres, we rounded a corner, there they were lying on their backs gasping for breath, the bunch majestically swept by never seeing again this illustrious pair. If anybody can shed any light on this, please let me know.

My own club Quintin one evening had organised a nocturn track meeting, the tract was in the centre of the village near the lake, being overlooked by the local chateau. Ron and I were pitted against no other than Rik Van Steenburgen and his partner in the Madison, the track was very tight despite being a little banked on the corners. Needless to say, this was no problem to Rik who would ride anywhere for money. Neither was it to me with my experiences on the tracks in South Yorkshire, but I did not like this one very much. Ron did not find it too easy; he was the same when he had given the track his best shot in South Yorkshire. A club mate Raymond Gautier being stupid enough to ride with road length cranks, then fell off breaking his collar bone; fortunately, not taking anybody else off with him. Among the publicity produced were bullfighting type posters, with of course RIK's name on top as the principal matador with in third place NEALE COE. The event was organised on the usual lines with the final event being the Madison; in this our main opponent was Rik who had a partner not quite as good, probably only a national champion, so we thought we had a chance. Our tactics were to put Ron in position for the sprint every time, whatever we did we could not beat Rik. Not a surprise to anyone but us. Normally, the stars would give a few crumbs to the locals, but not Rik. Not all the stars were this way, except perhaps Raymond Polidor, Poupou was, according to his teammates, which perhaps explains why he had so many second places.

As one would imagine equipment was not of today's standard, resulting in many causes of anguish. In one race going downhill on a bumpy road, my front wheel was doing gyrations from side to side, stopping as quickly as I could I discovered my forks were broken, easy solution new forks. Another occasion my frame was cracked, forking out for a new frame did not appeal. Pierre had the answer, "Bring the bike round to the plant tomorrow morning around 11.30 am, ask for me on the gate, they will expect you and bring you to me." Saint Brieuc Loco Plant was almost as big as the Doncaster works. They had the answer by welding this puny frame, which was completely dwarfed by the massive locomotives. On asking Pierre who I paid for this excellent reparation, the answer was, "We are all going into the bar just outside the works at lunch time, you are paying." In Brittany, one drink leads to another, no training that day. Another day, my chain broke just going into a corner, someone pushed me out of the way into the cornfield in full growth; I freewheeled back in the bunch the other side of the corner, just like a Monty Python sketch, no money that day.

One day, I was having my customary lunch in my first year's lodgings restaurant, at Boulevard Charner when two of the local police came in, asking if I was Neale Gordon, everyone knowing I was, I had no option but to agree to their request to come to town centre headquarters at 11.30 am. I knew it would not take long as I knew they would want to go for their aperitives at 12 on the dot. Despite not knowing what they wanted, I was not too concerned; they were also smiling or what passes for a smile with the St Brieuc flics. On arrival, Ron Coe and Sean Ryan were stood in a line against the wall, "Stand over there," I was told. "You have not renewed your visas, have you?" Addressing us all, "I have not thought about it," I said.

"Well, you can go if you sign these papers to leave France in 24 hours," they said in English; normally, the French will not speak English unless their life depends on it. We were quite surprised, but not prone to argument because they had guns. I was completely unperturbed as I thought I can pass a pleasant day in Jersey getting my passport stamped, which solved the visa problem for another 6 months. After that, I did not see Ron while later in the year, Sean never came back. At that time, the airport at St Brieuc had flights everyday direct to Jersey, so it was easy obtaining passage straight away.

Dressed as if I was just going for a business meeting, with no luggage, like I was to visit my Broker in St Peters Port, what a surprise greeted me on arrival; there were queues at the airport for flights, just like it was Christmas. Apparently, there was a seaman's strike of which I was completely unaware. For the moment I had a panic, just as if the policeman had drawn his gun, because I had a big contract for 2500 Fr. about 40 euros in today's money at the weekend, in a criterium of some importance, well for me it was. Doing my best to smile at the young thing in the booking office, I was probably nearly crying; I asked for a ticket on the next plane back to France. "Come back in an hour," she said, "you look as if your mother has just died." Success, I obtained a flight to Pleurtuit, Dinard, this landed at 7.00 pm. I had missed the last bus, so I set off to hitch hick back. After being ignored by many as if I was a hold up man with a gun, a big black Citroen saloon stopped, it was one of those you see in the old films with three rows of seats, one behind the other. To my surprise, it was full of nuns, after doing my best to explain the situation, they thought I was harmless enough, or perhaps they didn't. So, they invited me to climb in, spending the rest of the journey laughing and joking all the way back to St Brieuc. Maybe they put in an extra loop to keep me entertained or themselves out of the clutch of the mother superior. My contract money was duly earned at the weekend, Ron and Sean could not have had a contract or they would have been back.

Tour De France L'avenir 1961

At the end of June, it was off to ride in the British team of the very first Tour De L'Avenir. This was inaugurated in 1961 as a race similar to the Tour de France over much of the same course, setting off two hours before it's big brother. This was for amateurs and semi-professionals (Independents as they were then known). The race was created to attract teams from the Soviet Union and other Communist nations that had no professional riders to enter the T de F. I was to join up with the team at the Gare de Nord, Paris, then travelling by railway to the start at St Etienne. When I arrived at the station by train from St Brieuc, I found the team without trouble but did not have a good reception from the manager Bobby Thom, saying we did not know you were coming, if I could have found another rider I would. Rather shaken by this unexpected information, I replied that I went directly to St Brieuc from the Tour de Loire, the NCU were kept in the picture, I telegraphed them to say I would meet the team at the Gare de Nord as requested, to this, he had no comment.

The first stage St-Etienne to St-Etienne 145 km was very brutal at a very high speed, which I was used to coping with. Half way into the race, I was in the thick of things, bang on the wheel of a big Dutchman when we rode over one of those very low islands in the middle of the road that are hard to spot, flatting both wheels; the rear being ridable, I had a quick change for the front wheel, getting back in a chasing group. Disastrously further into the race on changing gear, the mechanism went into the rear wheel, worse still, the neutral service could do nothing to help me, so I was stood forlornly at the side of the road waving my bike. It was heart-breaking to see all the small group of riders passing, the race was smashed to smithereens by this time. It was even more galling to see another Mavic neutral service have a quick look at me, then pass on; I do not know how long I waited for a replacement; it seemed like an eternity, it had to be a long time judging by the number of riders that passed. In the first hour, 28.5 miles were covered, dooming the Welshman Davies to elimination, he had the very bad luck of puncturing in the first two miles.

After this dreadful start for me, I had to recover psychologically and put this behind me. Harry Hall who did a sterling job throughout the race was brilliant in putting my bike back together; his task was made a little easier by the fact that Simplex had replaced the entire teams Benelux gear systems with their own latest version, I only said a little easier, it was a very demanding job in a race like this. We did not have a British masseur; the tour organisers had found us one that normally worked for a French football team, to me not being used to such a luxury, he seemed to be on the ball. On the second day when we went over the first category Col de Porte, he gave us ephedrine to help our breathing in the high mountains.

Personally, I had never heard of ephedrine but some of the others in our team had; I do not know how helpful this was, there was no way of knowing. Ramsbottom rode magnificently on the Col de Porte, winning the finish on the track in Grenoble, taking the race lead. Alan should have started the third stage which climbed over the Col Du Mont Cenis to Turin, in the race leader's jersey. Regrettably, the night before the timekeepers had the overall result wrong, only the vigilance in seeing the error, and persistence in rectifying this by our manager Bobby Tom was able to obtain the correct result, but too late to obtain a race jersey to fit. Unfortunately, Alan lost the race lead on this stage, where the biggest crowds I have ever seen were packed like sardines at the side of the road, the next day back over the Alps into France was the same. Sadly, the Italian crowds were not the most supportive, they pushed their own riders up the climbs, even stealing the food out of my pockets.

It was claimed that the race reporters used little paper in making notes of the Big Tour whereas on our tour, it was claimed the notebooks were much used every day. One of the things I found the hardest in our tour was the long journeys from the stage finishes to the hotel; we could have been better organised with some food and drinks to eat on the bus. It must have been a logistical nightmare for the T de F organisers, which is no doubt why the dual race system was abandoned after a couple of years.

The fourth stage back into France finishing in Antibes-Juan le Pins after 3 cols. spectacularly saw the last 30 km along the coast from Nice to Antibes; we did not have much of a chance to admire the bikini clad girls adorning the route, a small treat for my birthday. Billy Holmes finished seventh; the rest of us finished together on the cinder track in Antibes except Warren Dalton who had spectacularly crashed on one of the mountain descents, his injuries were sufficient to have put a lesser man out of the race.

The fifth stage was 199 km to Aix en Providence; despite the almost tropical heat on this up and down route, I felt really good especially knowing that the finish was on the track; in my own mind I thought I could obtain a result, perhaps I was deluding myself, but I was up for it. I will never know if my confidence was misplaced or not as I was ordered to drop back. Bobby Thom apparently had a good reputation as a team manager, but he never had any discussion with me as to what I could contribute or anything else for that matter; it was as if I was just making the number up. Harry Hall, the mechanic was for more helpful, the only encouragement or advice I had was from Billy Holmes who had the pedigree plus the experience of two weeks stage racing.

On the sixth stage, 151 km a big loop around Montpellier, 28 miles were covered in the first hour Billy Holmes showed his metal finishing third at the finish. The next two stages were comparatively quiet with Pyrenees laying ahead.

On the ninth stage, finishing at Superbagneres, the first col was the third category climb of the col des Ares; then the second category col du Portillon on the Spanish side, with the Cabinaria military in their three-quarter hats complete with rifles lining the road, perhaps it was the sight of the rifles which discouraged the spectators.

On both these climbs, I was as comfortable as you can be climbing mountains; it was exhilarating dropping into Luchon where big crowds were waiting lining in front of the well photographed Spar hospital, shops and restaurants. From there, we set of to climb to the ski station at Superbagneres where the road rises 4000 ft in just 12 miles; I was well in touch, going fine then without warning, it was as if a curtain had dropped across the road and I had run into a brick wall, 50 or more riders must have passed me before I crawled to the finish. This also happened to much bigger fish than me, Gabica of Spain also blew nearer the top when he attacked too early; this undoubtedly cost him the overall race. Mario Cotti, the commentator found me lying almost dead on the grass, he was to talk about it in many of his commentaries, when I was competing, I often used to hear him using the word 'Phafalous Anglaise' (crazy, weird eccentric) when he was talking about me.

Not surprisingly, on the tenth stage to Pau even after a night's sleep and massage, I had dead legs the next morning being the first out of the back of the bunch after 4 km; then I hit the climb of the Tourmalet alone with the ambulance following me, my team had quite rightly given me up for a goner; eventually, I rode myself in catching a few other unfortunates then attaching myself to a bigger group on the climb of the Aubisque, finishing within the time limit which must have been quite generous. I now know I should have been eating less salad and more pasta, no one had spotted my bad eating habits.

Alan Ramsbottom finished a super second place on the 12th stage, the 42 km time trial at Limoges losing by 25 seconds to the Swiss rider Jaisli.

Finally, the last and 14th stage, Blois to the Parc des Princes, Paris 191 km. This was not a procession like the Grand Tour, 29 miles in the first hour 26 mph all the way. Everyone wanted to win this last stage; everyone thought they could which included me, *fools*! In the end, Billy Holmes was a magnificent second only being beaten by the 1-2 trick of two riders riding in collusion. Warren Dalton produced a great sprint from the bunch to take third place. Many said our race was much harder than the Grand Tour, attacking was none stop, the exuberance of youth.

The well merited general classification winner was the Italian Guido de Rosso by 38 seconds from Gabica of Spain, the finishers in our team were Alan Ramsbottom, Bill Bradley, Billy Holmes, Jim Hinds, Warwick Dalton, Gordon Neale, Hugh McGuire. Let's not forget, Felice Gimondi, Zoop Zoetemelk, Greg Lemond, Michael Indurin, Laurent Fignon, Egan Bernal, have won the Tour de L'Avenir, before going on to win eight Tours de France.

The finishing celebrations in the Grandiose Hotel de Champs de Elyse was something special; the champagne was scrumptious. I can still imagine seeing Jacques Anquetil the Big Tour winner walking down the corridor, a very finely tuned skeleton with muscles; he seemed more ordinary when I raced against him a couple of times in criteriums. Outside on the Paris streets, one could see plenty of military some in armoured cars, some gunfire could be heard. The background to this was the struggle of the National Liberation Front, FLN for the liberation of Algeria. It was at this time when the incident of the harsh repression of a peaceful demonstration of 30,000 people took place; in fact, it was much more than an incident, dozens of people were killed; some say it was many more, it is claimed many victims had their hands tied behind their backs and were thrown into the River Seine. It was Maurice Papon, the head of the Paris Police Force who ordered this diabolical repression, He was later convicted of crimes against humanity for his role as a Vichy collaborator in WW2.

Mid Auot Bretagne 1961

Back to Brittany and the criteriums, the first big event was a new race, the Mid Aout Bretagne with a new concept which perhaps the organisers thought was more attractive to the public than the previous Tour De Ouest. This was a series of eight criteriums one-time trial and one race on line, held between the 13-21 August, making the name appropriate; each individual criterium had its own classification, plus a general and points classification overall. All the best Bretagne's were riding plus others from further afield together with Raymond Poulidor; some of his team mates were riding in a variety of jerseys leading me to think naively they were all riding individually. Many years later, I was to learn by hazard that this was not the case, when riding as a veteran in a local race a spectator came up to me at the finish asking if I was the Neale Gordon of old, especially as I was old, it was not true, but I admitted to being he, yes, I thought so; he said I was in Poulidor's team in 1961, my job was to chase you down. Poulidor won two of the individual criteriums as Poulidor was not noted for being very generous with his team. I should have asked him if it was worth it, chasing me down.

In the second race at Plevin, I was fifth behind Poulidor and the ninth behind Simon Le Borne at Mael-Pestivien which moved me up to fourth on general in front of Poulidor. I held my place until a time trial at Saint Brieuc (on the circuit where famously Chris Boardman crashed out of the Tour in the prologue) with an on-line race of 90 km immediately afterwards to Perros-Guirec. Where disaster in the form of running out of steam, not unsurprisingly struck as could not resist riding in a track meeting at Guingamp the night before, as I had a contract. In retrospect, I should have withdrawn my thinking was that *a bird in the hand was worth two in the bush.*

After this, I had to wait until the last stage at the Mur de Bretagne to strike form again, this was a circuit with a long hill and a descent not flat. The Mur as it is known because of its climbs always attracts a stage in the tour whenever there are stages in Brittany. Early on, I was away with Francis Piplin, the climber who had successfully competed in the tour four times. Things were completely spoiled when my now ex-friend Ron Coe made a big attack bridging the gap, this was not so good as the Mafia would chase, not having confidence that their man could beat us both. Although the three of us continued to work together; Ron no longer had the legs, I was confident that I was stronger than both but careful not to make show it. Not surprisingly, we were caught with two laps to go, not before I had the pleasure of lapping Job Morvan and picking up some hefty primes. Poulidor jumped away to win when I was not positioned to follow, I finished seventh at 10 seconds, Ron ninth at 14 seconds with Piplin twelfth. Again, Mario Cotti had thankfully worked tirelessly whipping up the crowd, as I had a worthwhile sum to collect in the overall points classification.

We are now almost at the end of the season, there being what could be called the semi-professional championship of Brittany race, a Chateaulin with decent prize money. This was a race not open to professionals; when it was known I was riding this race, there were some rumblings that I should not be allowed to ride. No doubt, influenced by my good form in the Mi Aout Bretagne against the pros, no doubt also because I was English, some thought I should not qualify but I had a Committee de Bretagne licence. Nobody should have been surprised as my philosophy on earning a living was that I was not capable of just riding the big races all the time, when you could race three times a week, occasionally more in the busy season, it was prudent to make sure you picked up some money in the smaller races, not burn yourself out, which is a mistake I have seen some good young riders make; they do not think of their own limitations. My good form lasted on the day getting in a break of five or six riders; this being an on-line race finishing on the famous Chateaulin circuit. Feeling good with confidence to match, I attacked rather earlier than would normally be prudent, succeeding in picking up some important primes on the finishing circuit, nearly coming unstuck when I faded a little after this early attack, hanging on to the finish in the rain, another good job done.

Two or three more races to go, with a good end to the season, it was back to Swinton, South Yorkshire with enough money to buy a vehicle to get me to the races on my return the following year.

MAD HATTER BALLOON STORY

A very serious major event at the end of the year is the free wheel contest. At least it was to Dereck, the import one for the Doncaster riders took place from the top of Gringley on the Hill near Bawtry; Dereck's partner at the time was Margaret Allen, yes, the time trialist who entered the over-forty veterans road race championship; yes, to this day she is still disappointed she did not win, it was her equipment that let her down, she claims that she punctured. She is famous however in the time trialling world being prominently mentioned for her achievements in Beryl Burton's autobiography although they had one thing wrong it was her sister Maureen that made up the team in the 100-mile TT championship. She always beat Dereck in these contests; naturally, Dereck's Latin ego was offended, perhaps something to do with his having been a poacher at a younger age. As the years went by, he tried everything, swapped wheels, even swapped bikes, adjusted his weight, nothing worked; Margaret always won. Finally, Dereck decided it was the female anatomy that was beating him; finally, he competed with two large balloons stuffed down the front of his racing jersey; yes, it was that serious, URIKA, this was the answer; Dereck's prayers were answered he won.

Now, Dereck having discovered the competitive edge he was looking for, again he employed the balloons when he rode in the road race league, being satisfied he upped the ante in a big way by employing the same tactics in the week-ends 100-mile TT. Having warmed up using the usual massage creams, probably products from his pet shop, shaved his legs and chest, he liked to unzip his jersey at the front if it became too hot. Still, he had a very big hurdle to overcome, no other than Frank Mintoe was on the starting line, a noted stickler for the rules, if he had been a politician (he might have been), he would be classified as an archetypal Rees-Mogg, type right wing figure. By a stroke of good fortune, he overcame this formidable barrier; he claims he was up on his previous performances at the 50-mile mark. Then, a terrible catastrophe occurred-the balloons burst; he should not have shaved his chest. HE SHOULD NOT HAVE SHAVED HIS CHEST!

Amateur Road Racing and Tom Simpson Before 1960

I was 18 when I rode my first ever road race in 1956; this was organised by Dearne Wheelers, won by my friend Dave Stables from the same club which I was later to join. This then being a National Cyclists Union event (NCU) and was the only road race I was to compete in under this banner. The merger with the British League of Racing Cyclists (BLRC) took place in 1959 and became the British Cycling Federation, now British Cycling. The NCU dated as far back as 1890. And the BLRC was formed in 1959, largely at the instigation of Percy Stallard, who wanted to promote bunch racing on the open road. There was a great deal of acrimony between these two bodies before they buried the hatchet with this merger. The other lot, the time testers (time testers are supposed to be a throw back in time, according to Dr Who, I won't argue) remained largely apart, as they do to this day. My recollections are Sheffield cyclists were predominately BLRC, apart from Dougie Bond who rode the track. Barnsley riders were mostly time trialists. East of Rotherham towards Doncaster, riders were predominately track riders.

Much of the racing we did was in the scenically glorious Peak District, largely on traffic free roads; we were so lucky in that era. Many of the races started up the scenic wooded Rivalin Valley. For me, it was it not too difficult to ride through Rotherham and on to the start in Sheffield. It is hard to believe that occasionally if the race start was further out into the Peak District, I could catch a steam train 300 yards from my house. The train went into Bamford station via Sheffield through a tunnel. Other times, we had races round the evergreen sporting circuit of Wentworth. The headquarters for a long time being the appropriately named Cottage of Content pub, practically on the door step; I had workmates who used to walk their dogs on parts of this circuit, making a change from the usual sheep, we had as spectators. Other times, we ventured further afield such as the Telegraph and Angus 4-day event, where half the field walked over Fleet Moss or somewhere else once, because of the gale of a headwind.

The hardest race I can recall is when some moron organised a 3-lap race over the Jawbone and another climb equally as tough, two laps were enough; there were only a handful who finished the race. The same Jawbone near Stockbridge that the Tour De France recently rode over only once; of course, they had better gear and equipment than we had, even so, it was not as easy as you might have thought. Another race that had some really tough climbs was the Buxton 2-day that Bill Bradley won, the Burbage race over Burbage Moor was easier after that one. Back towards Maltby, the Brodsworth race promoted by Arthur Maxfield was an easy affair; perhaps, that is why I won in a bunch finish. In the Peak District when the weather was good, it could be fantastic; other times, especially when it rained, it could be miserable. Spare a thought for my friend Laurie

Rissbrook on such a day, who came into Tideswell on his own; at that moment, the only humanity in sight, I am stretching the word, stepped out of the shelter of a shop doorway, booking him for failing to stop at a halt sign; result a two-week ban from racing. Don't complain about Radar cameras after that.

Normally, I had a banana and dried fruit in my back pocket for the longer tougher races. For me, running out of energy when I was in a good position in a race was not uncommon; of course, I later realised I was not eating properly. Since I returned to racing in the UK after my time in France, as I had learned to eat correctly, this was no longer a problem; of course, lack of training was another thing. On one occasion on the run back into Sheffield, I blew up big time near Lady Bower Dam; on seeing a clubmate, I raided his saddlebag for the crumbs in the bottom.

Two well-known characters at that time were Sid and Jim Wilson; they had a bike shop in City Road Sheffield, sponsoring Ron Coe for a couple of years, as an Independent before he went to France. Jim ran the bike shop, Sid building frames in the back in his spare time. Jim was one of the few genuinely nice people in the world being a slow thinker and hesitant in his speech, but not lacking in any respect, rather to the contrary when you knew him better. I concluded that his comportment was as a result of being left behind as a rear guard at Dunkirk; he returned to the UK six months later via France; his family never knew exactly what happened. Sid is a real character, he had a wire brush fastened behind his saddle, no not to hit dogs with, though he might have done, but to rub his frame down afterwards, if it rained. Another character was Spanky McFarlane, no doubt gaining this nickname, as he was going to give everybody a good hiding in the race next week. Another personality, as well as being an elegant looking rider in his orange-coloured racing kit, was Dave Orford. It was he himself who had organised the sponsorship with Ovaltine, recruiting a team of independents. Dave always claiming at the finish he had been waiting for a sprint finish; of course, a sprint finish was rare over the terrain we rode. The joke being he was asleep again in the bunch, having drank too much Ovaltine beforehand. He proved his real capabilities later by becoming an accomplished time trialist (I would like to know what changed his philosophy so drastically, to him the TT word was worse than swearing). Then winning the World's Veteran Road Race Championship at St Johanne Austria in 1986 at the age of 56; I am told it was not in a sprint finish.

I was to witness at first hand, the abilities and unique qualities that Tom Simpson possessed, on the very difficult hilly Troway circuit in the Staveley area, which was promoted by Dick Aldridge on the 13 April 1958. Not surprisingly, Tom started as favourite for this race that finished on the cinder track at Staveley. Russ Foster, who was to become noted as a specialist in the Hill Climb races at the end of the season, was up the road in a two-man break with myself. Tom apparently biding his time in the bunch punctured. Tom having regained the bunch, then set about reeling us in; he was soon on his own. After what was said to have been a long hard difficult chase, he duly made contact. It appeared to us that he was in a bit of a state; in fact, he looked terrible, he must have thought we looked fresher than we felt. Rather than take any chances on the track finish, he put in a big successful attack on the last climb before the stadium. He had found something from out of the depth that only he could do, I have never seen anybody hurt themselves as much as he could. There was nothing we could do, Russ and myself came into the stadium 200 yards behind. There was only going to be one result from that, I could say I was once second to Tom Simpson.

The amalgamation of the two bodies went particularly smoothly as far as we the riders could tell. There was still a feeling that BLRC riders were the cream at road racing, especially the Independents. Like all the British cycling regions, we had regional championships. The road race was held over the moors on the outskirts of Sheffield, the organisers being the old guard of the BLRC. At the finish, there were only four or five riders contesting the sprint to win; I was well placed to come round to the right of Barry Trippet, there being plenty of room; unfortunately, Barry took me over nearly into the wall at the right-hand side of the road, cutting me off. Without doubt, he should have been disqualified in any normal circumstance. After deliberation, the judges came to the conclusion that Barry would be the independent champion, I would be the amateur champion, no disqualification needed.

The only foreign experience I had of racing abroad before going to France was like many others the trip to the Café den Engels in Gent. For me and my two mates, Dave and Barrie this was quite an experience; Gent we liked but not the horse meat served in the restaurant, we still have the cry of-A L BEAR RR, ringing in our ears after all these years, when Albert's mother had need of him. Tramlines and cobbles (PAVE) made for very tricky racing, couple this with the speed, making it not to the taste or advantage of the many British who gave it a try. Unlike France, entry on the line was accepted; Albert used to arrange the races for us. He came to me one day saying, "We have a race in Holland tomorrow. I am one rider short for the team, you are in the team, here is your Belgium jersey." In reply, I said, "It won't work; I cannot speak the language."

"Just stand in the middle and keep your mouth shut," was the reply. The Flemish are all big lads, so I was out of sight. The race was not like a Belgium race at all, but a criterium; to the delight of Albert, I had the best result of all finishing fifth. He was even more pleased when he peeled off his cut from the winnings, giving me the rest. My two companions who had ridden as Englishmen had abandoned the race. We found Dave eating an ice cream with a very attractive young Dutch lady on a bench in the park, having to drag him back to the bus with difficulty.

Third Year in France 1962

Before I went for a third season's racing in Brittany, Easter being early this year; it was my great pleasure to race at the Easter track meeting at Fallowfield Manchester. I had illusionary dreams of winning the Moratey Trophy in the scratch race. The then Ayatollah at Fallowfield, Jim Paterson had other ideas, by putting me in a 2-up pursuit with a Dutch pursuit champion. It would have been easier riding with Norman Sheil, but I think, he was saving him for the big one. I can tell you it was not like jumping on Hugh Porters wheel in a road race; he crucified me, I hardly came through at all. Afterwards, Jim said matter of fact, "I did not think you would be able to hang on."

During the winter, I had passed my driving test, buying myself my first ever vehicle a Morris 1000 van. My Uncle Laurie who worked at a garage after passing the entire WW2 as a Lorry driver and mechanic in some of the worst conditions imaginable in the Far East, North Africa and Europe, assured me that this van would be very dependable. As you can imagine, this vehicle stood out to the French; very soon, the local police knew who was driving it; very regularly, I was stopped at Malacoff roundabout, going into St Brieuc. They were quite rare, the roundabouts, at this time before the

English disease took hold. Originally, in my stupidity, I thought it was for speeding, they always said, "slow down, slow down," no doubt, they were taking the mickey out of my van. They have a sense of humour after all.

Eventually, I realised I had a sort of fan club with the police as they stopped me every weekend, wanting to know how I had performed in the race; I could not have been doing too badly or they would have stopped asking me. A surprise for my uncle, my van broke down-the pistons were worn out, perhaps, I had been going too fast after all. It is very difficult especially now, for me to believe that I actually striped the engine down to change the valves, which my uncle had sent out from the UK. Not surprisingly, I could not work out the sequence of the timing to put them back. My fans at my lunchtime restaurant persuaded one of their mates to fix the pistons; again it was drinks all round, but I went training this time, the rest went back to work.

On my return, I had been quick to see my club secretary at Quintin, to draw the rest of my winnings from the previous year. I learned that there had indeed been an attempt to block my winnings at Chateaulin, but that this had been quickly overruled and I had been paid. Some good news, I had been selected to ride in a French team in the Tour of Poland organised by Andre Leguioux. Apparently, there were diplomatic tensions between France and Poland. Andre, ever the enthusiast, had seen the opportunity to send an unofficial French team. He had asked me, he said, because I did better in the Tour L'Avenir than the Bretagne's; it was a mistake he said to send criterium riders, I said nothing, I was one.

At one race where again, Mario Cotti was the speaker, there was a rider's strike, the riders refusing to start on time.

This dispute had been rumbling on for some time, as in a few of the top criterium's the stars-Anquetil, Stablinsky, Simpson etc., received starting money, the rest Zilch. The Mafia were quite rightly the instigators saying without the rest of us, there would be no race. Before the race, the police got wind of the trouble, blocking spectators from coming into the village to watch the race. No cash to collect for Mario Cotti, no primes, no winners on this day. It was all later resolved to the rider's satisfaction, excepting many received fines for their part in the dispute; I was lucky, the Committee de Bretagne did not fine me, wrongly thinking I was an innocent party.

During the year, I had three invitations to ride on the track, but I should take the opportunity to tell you of the successful career of my first-year friend Georges Le Bouris. His style of riding reminded me in many ways of my older clubmate; the track sprinter Albert Thorpe. George was one year older than me; he worked full time as a telephone engineer, as a sprinter not training full time, he got away with his lack of stamina. On the track, he was something special with a list of victories over Darrigade, Guignard, the champion of France, Rousseau the Olympique champion R van Steenburgen, which pleased me. Finally, he made the most of his talent becoming a professional in the years 1967-72 making a very good living mostly in the criteriums.

Each summer, many of the Bretons, myself included went to race at two good-paying races conveniently placed in the middle of the week at Bordeaux. Always the same result, you encountered one by one the Bretons handing their numbers back at the headquarters. Always the same story; it was too hot for me, they never admitted the race was also too long, but ever hopeful we kept trying.

Wherever I have been racing over the years, France, Belgium, Austria, Mallorca, Luxemburg, there were three riders in particular who always turned up. One was the evergreen Bob Maitland who no doubt knew the scene better than me, another was Doug Collins; the third was Dave Orford. One day, Dave who had come out as usual to see what's what, getting some leisure time as well, found me saying he was staying on the camping at the Plage at Cesson. He said its great I can go down to the beach to collect my own mussels which taste nice, but he cannot understand why no one else is collecting them. When I told him there was an isolation hospital on the cliffs with an outlet to the beach, he went a funny colour; he moved to the municipal camp site in St Brieuc after that.

A few British riders managed to comply with entering races in advance, coming to race in their holidays. They almost invariably found they could not adjust to the differences in style, better bike handling with higher speed, they just did not have enough time. Some quite readily adapted to the less attractive of French habits, by urinating everywhere without much thought or consideration. The French are not as bad nowadays in this respect, although old habits die hard. At one particular race, the headquarters were at the Town Hall where there was a colourful arrangement of the town's best flowers in plant holders, just in front of the mayor's window, two British riders decided to relieve themselves watering the flowers. When in full flow, the windows opened, a very cross lady accused them of trying to ruin the mayor's special flower display that he was very proud of. In this era, there was not the abundance of botanic displays you see nowadays; the Bretons were more practical through necessity growing vegetables instead.

Other foreigners could behave badly; also, even distinguished ones, no other than the Eagle of Toledo, Fredrico Bahamontes. At one race, he was trying to fight the organisers because they refused to pay him his full contract fee. He was in poor form, but did not try to improve his form by finishing the race, taking the easy option by climbing off. Apparently, he had done the same in the previous race, so understandably less work, less pay. It was distressing to see a climber climbing off, not climbing down. There was a sort of hilarious side to this as Fredrico was not capable of fighting anyone; he was like one of Lowry's matchstick men, a puff of breath would have blown him away. Ron and John Geddes spent one racing season staying in the Perroquetvert Hotel (Green Parrot Hotel) slap bang in the centre of St Brieuc. They thought it funny to teach the staff bad language as well as the parrot; the problem was that the staff thought what they had learned was acceptable English. The guests found the air blue not green. As far as I know, the parrot was much better behaved. Nowadays, the hotel has been demolished to make way for a new development; I think the parrot flew away; it could not stand the bad language.

Back to the racing, I had crashed in June but was back to racing again in July, towards the end of the month. I was 12th in a Pro criterium against Poulidor, Anglade, Wolfshol Charlie Gaul etc. Then at the start of August, I was tenth in another Pro criterium against Simpson, Darrigade etc. Perhaps, things were looking better for the forthcoming Mid Aout Bretagne, which for the second year was the same format with different venues; I certainly made no arrangements to ride anywhere else at the same time. This time, Vin Denson and Brian Robinson were also competing. Brian was staying with his wife and family at Binic, so I arranged to travel to the races with him. First event, I was unplaced in a sprint for fourth place, second day, I broke a gear cable finishing in the bunch on a bike too small. Next event, half way to the race, the engine of Brian's car blew up; we then had to ride to the race on our own bikes arriving shattered for a nine-km time trial before the main event. Afterwards, I had a lift home returning in my trusty Morris 1000 van to tow Brian's car a fine looking two tone green Riley saloon back to Binic, arriving back home at 2 am. Brian managed to finish the afternoons on-line race. I was an abandon, neither Vin nor Brian pulled any trees up as I remember, but as Grand Tour riders, they saw things through to the end.

As well as riding a bike, Brittany had many other pleasures to offer; as well as a little swim from time to time at Le Rossaires Beach, I did a little fishing. Pierre had a small boat which we launched occasionally at the Port of Brehec, just up the coast from St Brieuc towards Paimpol. Pierre's main preoccupation apart from dropping a few lobster pots near the rocks in the bay was in laying out a long net held up at each end with a buoy and weights at the bottom, hoping to catch sea bream. Also, we had fishing rods to catch mackerel but the line was the piece de resistance. One day, a large grey vessel which looked very military appeared entering the bay; as Pierre's eyesight was not very good, he asked, "What does it say on that boat?"

"Marine National," I replied; "Putan, merde allors," was the response, "take these rods we are fishing for mackerel."

Afterwards, he said, "It's a good job they did not come any closer; these long nets are illegal, you know." Of course, I knew but you cannot say anything to a Breton; they thought these laws applied to Parisiennes not to them. At that time, apart from professional fishermen, only a few locals fished there, not the numbers of today. There is less fish now; the really big crabs cannot be found anymore. In Le League, the port of St Brieuc, it would have been hard to find a single leisure boat; today, you cannot obtain a mooring.

End of Year in Brittany 1962 and Now Back to UK

At the end of the racing season, I had to take stock seeing where I was going in the future. I had just discovered I had tape worms which had affected my form; this was easily treated and was not significant in my decision. What was apparent, I had not prepared well enough in the previous winter; *did I go to try the early season races in the south of France or did I go back to Swinton where I had a girlfriend?* My thought was I had seen the best of cycling based in Brittany not travelling all over Europe which has its disadvantages. Many of the best Bretons preferred to stay at home, rather than be paid modest wages as part of a team. Only the team leaders, the stars made really good money. Considering everything, having gained enormously in confidence by earning a living, although a modest one for three years by my own endeavours I chose to return.

I should not close this chapter without highlighting some of the other British riders who had spent some time racing in Brittany, some have already been mentioned. Ron Coe came over with his wife and baby for his third year staying on a camp site. He collected some prize money and after trying two or three races, he decided he did not have the form that he had when winning the National Road Race Championship four times, remaining for a holiday. One of the most successful riders of the British contingent was Alf Howling, based in Lorient; I believe he married a French girl in the end. The French press could never spell his name correctly in the results, when I saw him at various races, we used to about it. I would say, "I saw Mr Uglug finished fifth at wherever he raced last week." The French don't do H In 1959 Tom (Simpson) was signed by the French professional road racing team Rapha-Gitane-Dunlop, otherwise the place would have gone to Alf. Bad luck Alf Two compatriots from Sheffield Alan Huntington and Mick Coup were based at Loudeac for a couple of years; why they chose Loudeac I don't know, too far from the coast for my liking. My old friend the ever-enthusiastic Doug Petty lived with his wife in a caravan at Quimper; certainly a more agreeable place than Loudeac.

They say all good things come to an end; they did not for me as the Bienvenu's became my adopted family as I have no close English relatives. This is an even closer bond since I have been permanently resident here for close to 20 years, spending considerable time before that in my holiday home, neither has it been an end to my racing here.

On the ferry back to the UK, I ran into an inquisition from the Customs and Exercise who were on board. Not being many passengers, there was no escape from a thorough customs inspection, in reality more of a grilling. They must have thought I was smuggling contraband, or perhaps they knew more than me what drugs they thought the dastardly successful French pros were taking. Finding nothing, they concentrated their efforts on whether I had paid import duty on the two cycles I had with me. This appeared to be a ploy of some description; I did not tell them I had sent my track bike back direct to the UK by delivery service. **You would be correct in thinking I did not vote for Brexit.**

Back from France: Now Home for Good?

Looking for Work and New Professional Racing Licenses

When I had left school at 16, I joined British Steels staff training scheme working at the mighty Templeborough Steel Complex, meeting people in the extraordinary setting of the colossal furnaces, finding my way round, making sure I did not become incinerated was ok. While I was there, someone was entirely consumed by the molten steel in the furnace, they had to say some iron stud in his shoe, that was the remains for burial; it was no use having him cremated; was it? The rest was boring in the least. Consequently, I changed career directions completely, obtaining employment as a trainee laboratory assistant at a Coal Tar Distlers in my home town, despite the fact that I had never done physics and chemistry at school. You would not expect that I had, I had gained a scholarship to a technical college at the age of 13 enrolling in the commercial course. My new employers optimistically enrolled me in day release and night school; I suspect there were no other applicants for the job.

However, I was not out of place spending four years covered in tar products, a bit like Brrr Rabbit, the pinnacle of my learning is that it seems to be a shame to burn coal. I said I was not out of place because it certainly was an educational upheaval moving from a Secondary Modern School in a mining area to a technical college, as in my case, I had passed the examination from a next to bottom grade class, astonishing the teachers; the headmaster said they had failed dismally and in order to catch up with my education, he suggested they keep me for another year; fortunately, my parents quite rightly would have none of this. Well, I left with some good results, book-keeping and geography as you would expect included. I did Pass my GCE in English language to the surprise of my tutor; however, you can judge from reading this book if he was wiser than the examiners.

On my return from France, I could see that my future lay as a sales representative. Redifusion the TV relay company were looking for salesmen, this turned out to be selling cable TVs where they had a network, the bonuses for sales seemed good; not having many options, I took the job. Who did I meet on my first day at work? None other than my previous clubmate at Quintin; none other than Bronco (Ron Coe) who also was on cavaliere for greener pastures. We were both given different areas to work. I worked out that the best way to operate was to find out where the reception for TV was not good, a bit of door knocking worked wonders. It was too easy I could meet my targets in a few hours; I did the intelligent thing just exceeding my targets without showing that the target was too easy.

Consequently, I looked for extra work, becoming recruited into a company called Ideal Carpets selling carpets direct, my modus of operation was putting out leaflet's door to door; following up the replies, I went and sold the carpets. Becoming quite successful, I recruited other salesmen until I had a team, the bosses rented me an office in central

Doncaster near the Danum Hotel. Not surprisingly, I kept the two jobs going together for some time; Ron meanwhile took a rep's job with a chemical company.

Meanwhile, I continued to race, riding the local races which at that time were often in the absolutely fantastic racing area of the Peak District with an occasional race on the sporting Wentworth Circuit. Having an independent license, I was supported morally more than financially by the Wilson Brothers who had sponsored Ron before he went to France. I am told he is still racing, perhaps having formed a special age category in the veterans racing; no, I am not joking. I believe there is an over 80 categories now. Why not? After all, in France, they have recently created an hour record in the over 100 categories, especially for a Frenchman Robert Marchand. He recently went on to create a record of 22.547 Km at the unbelievable age of 105.

In cycling, there was a bombshell to fall for independent riders like me; we were defunct, none existent, done away with, obsolete like the Dodo, there were only going to be amateur or professional riders. This was because the world's cycling bodies had caved in to pressure from the Olympic movement. In my opinion, the semi-professional class worked very well in cycling at that time. Naively, the Olympic movement thought that this re-classification would preserve their amateur status as if there was one. Many years later, they stopped deluding themselves by admitting professionals.

Finally, when the crunch came in 1965, I applied to be reinstated as an amateur; as far as I was concerned my professional ambitions were over when I came back from France, my application was turned down full stop, no appeal, Nada as the Spanish would say. Later, the nonsense I was given was, "we need riders like you to make the professional class work." I did not see it that way, reluctantly rather than give up racing I had no choice but to take out the license. My ever-enthusiastic friend Doug Petty did not hang about; he arranged sponsorship for a team with Croad Automatics. Doug knowing, I had no choice but to take out a license wrongly assumed I would want to be in the team. As he had agreed the supply of bikes from Ellis Briggs and knowing my dimensions, he had included me in the order. Hopefully, he understood my reasons for not wanting to commit myself to the obligations that went with being in a team. This was not an easy decision; in order to have the best racing results, you need the support of a team. Despite my refusal to be in the team, Ellis Briggs proceeded to give me the cycle-a very nice machine it was under trade name of Favori, my gratitude goes to them. As I was by now an established CIS insurance agent, I sponsored myself under this name as a promotion of my business. I did not receive any comment from the chiefs at the CIS; I suppose they were very indifferent. In addition, I had some limited equipment sponsorship from Henry Holmes Cycles in Rotherham while continuing to race on my red Favori machine.

Back to the racing, I cannot say other than that I did enjoy the racing in the beginning helped by the break from the insurance job. This first year, Goz Goodman who was a year younger than me, won about everything, he had 11 victories that year racing for Viking Trumann Steel. He certainly had the magic formula, that deserted him the following years never to return, or he gave up the magic formula. In the three years I rode as a professional, it was almost the same opposition in every race on almost the identical course as the year before; this of course was one of the problems in the UK professional class, it was almost like a theatre group going round each year to the same locations. There were some exceptions of course; one was the Vaux International Grand Prix of 1967 where I was to meet Michael Wright, for the first time since the tour of the Loire and Cher in 1961; he still did not speak English. This was a very tough race over the Northumbrian Moors taking in the climbs of Hill End and Bollihope four times each, not the race for a sprinter which Michael was noted to be. My tactic in this race was to stay with the leaders as long as I could on the climbs, without killing myself; then, when Hugh Porter caught me up on the descents to jump on his wheel getting back near the front, this worked to a limited extent, my finishing 13th. Michael incredibly enough showed his real class by winning.

Whenever I had the opportunity to go to St Brieuc, I took advantage staying with my adopted family. Whilst there, I raced in the local races for my old club VC Quintin with whom I obtained a license; this would have choked the people who refused my reinstatement as an amateur, but, "Fuck Them," I obtained an amateur license. To ride professional races in France was too much to ask. Being well known to most, I was accepted, even welcomed, no one was complaining, I came back from my holiday fitter than when I went.

Pro Race Isle of Man and Tom Simpson's Demise

Another race that was out of the ordinary was the Pro race in the Isle of Man, in the late 60' s things must have been getting better, the prize money was huge. The Manx Tourist Board, who must have had a colossal budge invited all the top continental pros to ride. Owing to a last-minute airline strike the pros were not all arrive, scenting that I had a real chance of picking up some of the available dosh for the lower placings I decided I should ride. On telephoning the race supremo a Manxman, Curwen Clague I was told it was no point in entering for the race as transport was impossible. Eventually after some lengthy procrastination he agreed if I could make it, I could ride. Manxmen are a bit special; Steve Jocking another Manxman was a larger-than-life character who I later knew well on my training camps, not for nothing he was known as the pocket rocket. Not being as stupid as Curwen thought, I had learned that there was an airbridge for the cyclists who were booked in for the cycling week. No tickets were available, completely impossible so I was informed. Nothing in life is completely impossible, so I went to the aerodrome at Blackpool where long lines of cyclists were waiting to board a Dakota aircraft. The organizers were shouting names out, people were putting their hand up and boarding the plane. I waited until there was no response, on putting my hand up I boarded the plane, job done, only thing to do was to pay for the return ticket.

No benefits were obtained from my endeavours, early in the race I punctured after a wheel change, I was struggling to return to the bunch with none other than Rik Van Looy, the wrong man on a climb to get you back on, he looked overweight to me, poetic justice in the end.

In 1967 I again visited the Isle of Man Pro race in what proved to be Tom s last race in the IOM.

I saw Tom before the race, I was rather shocked by his appearance, he looked very unwell being more than usually drawn in the face, with a grey pallor. I said to him what on earth has happened to you, he replied I have had flu, my training was behind but I am OK now. You don't look OK to me I said, then no word of a lie, I told him if you do not look after yourself and continue like this you will kill yourself. At the time, even when I heard of his death, I had no idea what a prophesy this was, my first thoughts were that he had crashed on a mountain descent into a ravine. Unbelievable he went on to win the race for the second time.

It was an evening whilst riding on the chain gang, that I heard of Toms death, someone shouted from the side of the road, "Simpson's dead." On learning the details, I should not have been surprised but all the talk was of doping. In my opinion, it was for more complicated than that. Probably, the start of the sequence was in the winter of 1966, when Tom broke his leg in a skiing accident badly enough for the physician to say it would probably be the end of his cycling career. Tom being Tom, was having none of that; his determination was to prove the doctor wrong. Tom in his own mind was convinced that 1967 was his best chance of winning the tour with its huge financial rewards; there being no doubt that money motivated him very much. His abnormal powers of digging deep into his depths, even by the competitive abilities of most top athletes was extraordinary. His demise was not helped by some sort of flu he said had infected him when we meet in the IOM.

It was widely assumed that amphetamines played their part which I cannot confirm or deny; to my own knowledge, they were widely taken in competition at this time. I tried them once myself; fortunately, they made me sick so that was the end of that. This was my good fortune, as many of the French riders who beat me, who I knew were doping have since died of heart attacks. I am not saying that everybody I knew that died with a heart attack was doping, but rather a few I knew did, too many for sure. It was well known that amphetamines kill fatigue and hunger, also blocking the elimination of toxins that can provoke a profound coma. It was speculated that other products contributed, that was not necessarily the case. One thing was sure, it was not normal that a man of 30 died while doing what was after all a sport, even if it was an extraordinary tough one at that.

As I went through Harworth the week before, I never expected to come back again so soon; especially for a funeral, Tom's funeral. At the funeral, the turnout was fit for a king, which in his own way he was; there were more people at the funeral than the total numbers at the weekends football matches. When I arrived, the church was full, the locals who recognized me, said, "I should go inside." I preferred to stay outside with the locals, keeping my thoughts to myself; I did not follow the procession the short distance to the local cemetery where he is still buried to this day. **What a sad day.**

In the three years, I only won one race, this was an event with a points classification, in a criterium. I did some reasonable rides, the big failing I had was that regularly I was up the road in the breaks, but ran out of steam. This was not surprising as I was not able to do the mileage for this type of racing. The chain gang we had at this time was full of talent. The list is too long, except to say, we had my clubmates from the all-conquering Rockingham Club, Mike McNamara, Ticker Mullins, Jonnie Blacker etc. Johnnie Blacker was the fastest. On Tuesday and Thursday nights, we assembled in Doncaster, going on the old A1 towards Bawtry passing the outskirts of Finningley Airfield, where in this epoch the V Bombers, Vulcans, Victors or Valliant's passed just above our heads in a thunderous catatonic roar. Like many things in life, we became accustomed to this traumatic din, not even thinking that they were carrying nuclear bombs, which they probably were, as it was the Cuban missile crisis.

From Bawtry it was on to Barnby Moor, Roach Abbey, Maltby, Braithwell. Despite Roach Abbey being in ruin, one visitor once asked me if there were still any nuns there, if you believe in ghosts; "yes," I replied. Quite a good contingent from the Rockingham Club met up some nights at the Gate Inn Pub in Swinton; I could not keep up with them at drinking, but I could more than handle them on the chain gang. Ticker Mullins had an excellent pedigree as a road man riding internationally, winning stages in the Tour of Britain, as well as being a pillar of the time trialling team; curiously, I never raced against Ticker. I guess it was a professional amateur divide, the divide did not end there; yes, I attended the annual dinner, applauding the brilliant results of the riders, Mikes BAR win, the national time trials championship wins, among others (by the way, Mike actually did more miles than Beryl Burton in the 12 hours championship; he slightly went off course, it did not count in his total mileage, Mike was too much of a gentleman to say anything officially). Never ever did I have even my name mentioned at the annual dinner, obviously to even think there was a professional in the club, was taboo, though I really wasn't one. I think it was down to the secretary, who was a fanatic time trialling fan, secretaries are much harder to find than riders.

I had the good fortune to have a retired aunty and uncle in the charming village of Haddenham where Roger Newton lived, the team mate of Goz Goodman in the Viking Truman team. Often, there were races in this area, where I was able to stay with my considerate and understanding relatives. My uncle was the retired manager of British Steels Rolling Mills at the Parkgate works near Swinton; his health was to suffer along with many others from the cocktail of the air-laden pollution at those works. Another reason why he was to retire further south in Buckinghamshire was to escape the persistent fogs at that time in South Yorkshire, thus prolonging his life a little. Nonetheless, I finally had enough of all the travelling to races up and down the country; I decided to retire. Not taking my machine out at all for another 10 years. Unlike the demise of the huge railway workshops in Doncaster and St Brieuc, together with the locomotives, which had run out of steam, I had some puff left, neither was I obsolete, more is to come after a 10-year wait. In the meantime, being just short of 30 years old, I thought I need to take up some other sport, **which**? Nobody much seemed to ride the bike at past 40 years of age at that time. Seeing that many older people played golf, I decided on golf. I enrolled at Hickleton Golf Club on the circuit where I had ridden my first ever road race, with the assistance of a former cycling club mate.

Starting in Business 1970

With not spending so much time training and racing, I now had the opportunity to spend more time in business. In 1970, I was still a CIS insurance agent; we had a strike which lasted 13 weeks. It being obvious to me that this was going to last for some time and in meeting a former racing colleague, Ray Levers who incidentally was fourth in the race that Tom won on the Troway Circuit, we talked business. He owned an insurance brokerage business in Barnsley which he managed. On raising the subject of a new innovative investment plan by a major insurer, it was agreed that this looked exciting; so, we agreed a business arrangement whereby I would market it to my clients rather than do nothing for the rest of the strike. This was successfully received by many of my clients; at the end of the strike on seeing a wider horizon of being able to offer better to my clients than was the case previously with a more productive future for myself, I had no desire to return to the CIS. What had been the most successful for me at the CIS, was my motor insurance account.

However, as an insurance broker, I could offer the best rates on the market, taking agencies with most of the competitive insurers including Lloyds of London. My plan was to open an office selling investment and life insurance as well. Things in life are rarely as simple as they sound, on stating to my boss at the CIS that I did not want to return; he pointed out I had no choice as we owned our own agencies at the CIS, who had given me a loan in the first place to buy my agency. Me being adamant that I was leaving, there was obviously deadlock; Ironically, the union that had called the strike in the first place became involved. On meeting with the management, it was agreed between them that I would come back to work to put my agency in order, they would then transfer the agency to someone else; subsequently, I would receive the cash balance for the sale of my agency. After giving my agreement, the big boss from Manchester head office came to see me, saying, "We do not want you to leave; we are offering you promotion." Thanking him, I replied, "I am leaving as soon as I can," which I did despite their endeavours to persuade me otherwise.

I opened a small front office in a secondary shopping area in Mexborough, to set up business. In due course, I recruited a part-time salesforce to train to sell the not too complicated modern open endowment insurance etc. Subsequently, I took over the whole building, as I needed the space. During which time I enjoyed playing golf, the contacts I made did me no harm at all. Mexborough was not the most prosperous of towns; I was not oblivious to the fact there were better opportunities elsewhere. When the opportunity came to purchase a predominant motor insurance broker in the centre of Garforth, I jumped at it. In addition, a very successful expansion was opening a Halifax Building Society Agency in Rossington, along with a new partner for that business. As commercial premises were completely lacking in this village, we set a precedence by purchasing a miner's cottage, converting it to our needs. Four out of five families in Rossington held accounts with the Halifax; now they had no need to travel into Doncaster for their banking requirements; we were very busy with three tills constantly in operation. Very soon, we opened a new Halifax Agency in a posher area of Doncaster, Edenthorpe which it would be as Jeromy Clarkson of *Top Gear* fame originally came from there; incidentally, I like his written humour more.

By this time, the investment and life assurance I transacted became controlled by the Financial Services Authority. All staff working in this field was strictly regulated, having to pass exams; this put an end to our part-time staff; many of them were firemen, so they still had good jobs. Now, we were qualified as Independent Financial Advisers as well as selling insurance. Being IFAs had a distinct advantage to our Halifax clients in that we offered a full range of investment products from the entire UK market. Unlike the Halifax, along with other banks and building societies that only provided a narrow range of providers, we unlike most other Independent Financial Advisers had the advantage of a substantial client base with our building society agencies.

Bike Out Again Sad Death Pat Bradley

During this time, I was still not riding my bike, but playing golf rather seriously. I became involved with club management, one attraction of golf is the 19th hole, to the uninitiated the bar. Despite golf being a walk of 8 to 10 km, I started to put on weight; even bending down was becoming an effort. Having decided to do something about it! You guessed it, I took the machine out and put some puff into the tyres.

During these 10 years, I was still actively in touch with my adopted family in France, going over at least once a year, often more, where they kept a room in reserve for us. Regrettably, we had one trip that no one could possibly have wanted. Pat Bradley who had lived in the next street to my parents was found dead in his room in St Brieuc. He together with a clubmate, Pete Smith from the Rockingham Club, had arrived only two weeks earlier in St Brieuc. Pete had returned home to collect his car, which had been undergoing repairs to bring it back, thus surviving. They knew of Tom's career starting in St Brieuc and myself having spent three years there; however, I was not involved or aware of any arrangements they had made.

It turned out they had been ill; the pair of them almost from the moment they had arrived to join a club in St Brieuc. This club had arranged for them to rent rooms in the town. Being new, they were not well known, apparently when appearing unwell, not too much attention was paid to it, as it was the flu season. Pat who was a very promising bike rider with a record to prove it was not the type to give in easily. Despite visiting the pharmacy for medication, no one suspected he had carbon monoxide poisoning, which was to prove fatal. An investigation found that a faulty room heater was the cause. It was my unpleasant task to accompany his parents Alice and Sid with his only sibling, an elder sister Anthea. My adopted family found accommodation for us, being a great help in meeting the authorities and all concerned. When the body was returned home, the entire cycling community of South Yorkshire walked the 3 km from Pat's home up the main street to Swinton Parish Church, blocking all the traffic for some time. This brought back memories of Tom's funeral to many, including myself. Pat's parents, particularly Sid, never really recovered from this devastating blow, it did not help to keep Pat's bike and belongings in his bedroom as a sort of mausoleum.

Nonetheless, we used to see them regularly, meeting also with a group of the Rockingham Club in the Gate Inn Bar in Swinton. Alice and Sid did their best to put this behind them. Unfortunately, this did not succeed for Sid who was very seriously psychologically affected succumbing to an earlier death. His situation was not helped by keeping all Pat's belongings in his bedroom despite attempts by others in his family to change this.

When two riders go together to try to make a career, it is not unusual for them to take different paths but thankfully not as dreadful as this. For example, Barrie Hoban and Bernard Burns went together to race in Belgium. Bernard, who some considered to be the better rider, came home; Barrie stayed, result, 10 Tour de France stage wins etc.

Meeting Georges in Canada and Florida

My friend Georges Le Lart from my first year in France, who had then gone to live in Montreal, kept in touch. We met often during our summer holidays in France, then several times at Christmas and the New Year in Florida when he drove down in his camper van, all the way in the winter, from Quebec.

As we had a golfing friend from back home who was resident near Clearwater, for six months, we sometimes stayed with them at this period, or nearby, often travelling and visiting much of the rest of Florida. As you would expect, I also hired a road bike whilst there. Regularly, I used to meet with a very large group on a Saturday at the library at Tampa and on a Sunday at her pier at Clearwater. These groups were spit into several sections, the very oldest riders did about 10 miles before stopping for a full breakfast, then returning, to the quickest group, which included several ladies, who also raced back at home and one Englishman, me. The route used to take us on the long straight wide boulevards, that are typical in this part of the world, where we could turn right on the red lights. The nosiest beings on these early mornings were the invading parakeets, chattering in the trees. It was only when we came to one of the many suspension bridges crossing the canals and waterway that we had any elevation. Quite easily, the best and most enjoyable part was when we reached the Fort DeSoto National Park, which enabled us to ride east, then west within the limits of the park with uninterrupted view over the Gulf of Mexico Ocean. Because of the mild climate, this was quite enjoyable, but a long way from what I was accustomed to in Europe.

You can imagine what I thought, on having a beer one day in the bar at the end of the pier in Clearwater with a rider from Chicago at the end of the ride, when he said, "Isn't it brilliant here for riding you bike?" My thought was *I am glad I don't have to ride a bike in Chicago,* but wisely, not wanting to strain Anglo American relations, I said nothing. I also kept my mouth shut when I met an immaculately dressed businessman in a classy hotel at Naples whilst we were both looking at the Muscovy ducks on the hotel lake. At that time, as I was not familiar with Muscovy ducks, I asked him if you could eat them. To my astonishment he said, "Only black people eat them." There was a cycling path that was independent of the road traffic that went direct to Tarpon Springs from Clearwater. This was one of the few places in the whole of Florida that I discovered was similar to towns in Europe; otherwise, it was take your car to the shopping mall. The problem with this bike track, as with many others was the very frequent need to cross a traffic laden road. My favourite place in the whole of Florida with any sort of European feel was without doubt, Key West. Unfortunately, cycling there was not possible. I did find a small club that had an arrangement where they met up in their cars and then proceed to an out-of-town destination to commence the ride, where the roads were quieter, but this still did not compare favourably with European roads.

Often with Georges and his wife, we went together to a restaurant. One day, we went to a super place in Key Biscayne, where we ate frogs' legs, not the little pathetic ones you occasionally can obtain in French establishments, but the rather scrumptious Everglades larger variety. This was at the time a very rural location which would be unrecognizable and unaffordable nowadays with the development in Miami. On another occasion, Georges said, "We have found a super place to eat you are in for a treat, follow us." We drove for what seemed like forever to arrive at an immense place with a car park to match. On entering, we discovered what was to be my first experience of an ALL YOU CAN EAT RESTAURANTS anywhere. This was full of very large people mostly of African origin and I do mean large as only Americans can be. There was an enormous selection of food of every type, just like you see in the best ones of this type today. Exactly like the well-known ones, you can find on the border between France and Spain, particularly the ones a Perthus. George and his wife left us for dead in the eating stakes, consuming an unbelievable quantity. A few days later, when we met, I said, "I cannot believe the amount you ate in the restaurant."

He replied, "We ate nothing at all for two days afterwards." There is very good; all you can eat Chinese restaurant nowadays in St Brieuc that I can certainly recommend.

In 1974, we accepted an invitation to visit Georges and his wife at the time of the World Road Race Championships in Montreal. Gratefully, we booked a flight. The day before the flight, the airline went bust; we had to book another airline, seems a familiar story; well, by the current shape of things, this will become **even more common**. On arrival at Montreal, the metro was suffering from the French disease, a strike, but no matter Georges had a French car. On the day of the race, it was oppressively hot, a bit like you can experience in Thailand or Singapore. I am glad I did not have to race in these conditions. We watched the French teams' heroic efforts from a hill by the university; this was a textbook lesson in tactics, first the opposition had to chase Francis Campaner, then Bernard Thevenet sacrificed his own chances trying to obtain a win for Poulidor. They reckoned without the invincible Edie Merckx. I was not going to tell POUPOU that at least he had further embellished his unfair title of the eternal second.

Joined Doncaster Wheelers Starting 1978

After I had taken my bike out of retirement, I joined Doncaster Wheelers as I now lived at Sprotborough, Doncaster. Riding leisurely at first, though still playing golf as well, it was 1978. Occasionally, I went to the Golf Club House in full cycling lycra, many of the members were tradesmen or worked at the local colliery. However, the president was in a fantasy world, thinking we should have the same standards as Gleneagles. Now, it is owned by Trump, no doubt standards have gone downhill. The president said to me, "You cannot come here dressed like that," to which I replied, "I can, I am the captain." His mouth remained firmly shut after that.

Things with cycling progressed slowly at first. Not before long, I joined the young hopefuls on the training rides. Whenever I made observations or suggestions how they could progress, like many youngsters they took no notice whatsoever. Inevitably, I started racing again; eventually, it was no surprise to anyone that my results were better than theirs. The outcome being, along with a good friend Dale Coen, we joined another club, the Dinnington. Not only did I join to race with them, I agreed to sponsor the club, initially as Ideal Insurance.

To start with, I only raced in local events. Becoming more serious as time passed, I started to race in the Peter Friar National Series. On an average, there were eight races during the season in different areas of the country. Your best five races were to count for a points system, with an overall winner in addition to the individual races. This series was for the riders over the age of 40. Later, a classification was to be introduced for the riders aged over 50, then later races for over 50s only. My first event was at Stevenage, won by Eddie McGourley from the North East. I was in a break of five riders at the finish. Yes, I was fifth, having ran out of steam, my stamina was to improve as I did more racing. I was to race in this series whenever I could, which depended on my being in the UK.

In the mid-week, we had the road race league, which was held on a different circuit each week. Four different circuits were used, the same four circuits the following month. Groups were set off on a handicap basis, more to do with ability than age. Of course, older riders like me could not match the rapidly progressing Russ and Dean Downing's of this world. They were not the only prospects in South Yorkshire, none the less when Dereck (the Mad Hatter) was in the front group; this group were difficult to catch. Frequently, they were never caught at all. I was not allowed to start in the front group. The back group started too fast for my liking, when they caught up, I was ok, being rode in. One year, when I finished second in one race, a clubmate Paul was rather indignant that I had not won, telling me to put an objection to the winner, as he a man (a few of the best ladies were also competing) was paced by a car. My reply was that this was not a good idea, as Adrian Timmis (the Tour de France rider and training camp stalwart) paced me behind his motor bike to try to catch him. Inevitably, as happened all too often, some good circuits had to be abandoned because of traffic problems. No such problems with the Wentworth Circuit. The wimps among the riders complained that the circuit was too hard, succeeding in having it changed for another one. I could not see much of a future for these complainants. After all, the best description of this course was as a sporting circuit. If they had been asked to race on the Jawbone Circuit, the hill as used in the Tour de France, then they might have had a justifiable complaint.

1994-1995 was the time of the miner's strike. The chain gang on which I was as regular rider as I could be, had to pass a police road block in the Bawtry area. This was set up to prevent a clash of the striking miners' pickets with those working from North Nottinghamshire. At first, we suffered the indignity of being put out of our rhythm by the suspicious police stopping us. Perhaps, they thought we were demonstrators with the cunning ruse of dressing as racing cyclists, to pass the picket line. After a couple of times being stopped, they worked out that what they saw was the genuine article, letting us pass.

I was a partner in a Halifax Building Society agency in Rossington, the striking area; 5 miles away, I was also a partner in the Harworth agency, the working area. Consequently, I was acutely aware of families who had relatives in both camps in the dispute, being split apart. Some to this day, have not been reconciled after all this time.

In the financial services industry, we were later to come under criticism by the government regulatory authority's for selling endowment policies with mortgages. What is not recorded is that many miners owned their own homes in our area, many of them had this type of mortgage. The endowments were a saviour for many families; they were able to withdraw money from them during this prolonged strike, of course you did not have this facility with a normal mortgage, for which they were grateful to us. Being independent financial advisers, we only used the top companies; many of the banks were restricted in their choice using companies, such as Eagle Star, who gave far from satisfactory results.

At the time we were riding through the police cordon, we had a cycling club colleague, Paul who was on the picket lines at Orgreave. There the miners were being brutally charged by the police on horseback, as witnessed on TV. O SS E S as Joe Marsh our secretary in the Dinnington would call them in his Kiverton Park accent. Undoubtedly, Paul was a mercurial character, whatever happened on those picket lines, he did not deserve the 3-year prison sentence he received. What was even worse, was when he came out of prison being unable to obtain employment, because he was blacklisted. As the police actions were well recorded as being open to question, despite the promises of the Thatcher Government for an enquiry, this never materialized. After many years of further promises, no action was taken, no prosecutions were brought, those responsible escaped justice. After what we have seen of the Hillsborough Enquiry with the same police force involved, an enquiry most likely would have produced the same futile result, with the guilty parties getting off scot-free.

Initially, my club the Dinnington, promoted a professional race based at Harworth. After a time, this was replaced by a series of League of Veteran Racing Cyclists events (LVRC) The first prize in this successfully well-supported event, was the prestigious trophy Tom had won in the Tour De La Ouest in 1959. The race finishing line was near the house where Tom's father lived, close also to the cemetery where Tom is buried. Dave Marsh, with help from Tom's cousin Chris Sidwells inaugurated a memorial museum to Tom in this village, which is easy to find and well worth a visit.

I was to ride in many LVRC events over the years, meeting many friends, rivals old and new. Some of the better races were organised by Dave Orford in the wonderful Peak District. Another was the sporting Wentworth Circuit, where Dogie Bond was to run popular and successful races. Often in order to be more competitive, I raced in an age group 10 years younger. I had more than my share of success in racing in a younger age group. Others racing successfully in a younger group, were Dave Nie and Ray Minovi among others.

During this period, among the open to all age's races, were several on the Notton Circuit at Wakefield. These were held mid-week during the lighter nights. Ken Cowdell also organised similar races on the Bishops Wood Circuit near Selby. It was in one of these races that the Mad Hatter put his theory of riding a fixed wheel bike to test. At first, all went well, although his results are not recorded. The second time, his chain jammed resulting in a near fatal accident, when he fell heavily on his head. At Leeds Hospital where he was urgently evacuated, things did not look so good, as he was given the last rites. Thankfully, he made a full recovery, to the great relief of all his friends, who were many. Thankfully, also for you, the readers of this book, which would be rather lacking without some of the further exploits of Dereck being recorded. It was only a couple of years later that Dereck had a further accident riding in a local race. This time although bad enough, it was not so serious, although he was taken to hospital in Scunthorpe. Being Dereck, there was a silver lining to this, in that he befriended the nurse who looked after him. As far as we knew, all went well for some time, then I had a phone call from a friend, asking if I had seen the news. The news was, Hatter had been arrested for attempted murder. This event was widely covered on the local radio, TV, and the local newspapers. In due course, I gleaned the full story.

The girlfriend had a house in Goole, Dereck's house and pet shop was in Askern. They shared their time between these two abodes. She apparently was a heavy drinker, who was rather difficult from time to time, it is impossible to imagine that Dereck himself was difficult. On the day of the arrest according to Dereck, she was uncontrollably inebriated. Needing to transport her home, the only way he could achieve this, was by locking her in the boot of his car. He was seen doing this, hence his arrest. Two nights were spent in the local Nick at Askern, whilst the local judiciary decided their next step; it was the local police sergeant who took the next step. Arriving on duty, seeing it was Dereck, his instructions were "Oh, its Dereck he is no trouble; let him out." In earlier years, Dereck was well known as one of the local poachers. He had once confessed to cooking a hedgehog, saying, it was not worth the effort as they did not have enough meat on them. The girlfriend who was unharmed did not press charges; consequently, the affair was dropped, I mean the charges were dropped, not the affair, she was to die of some nasty disease some years later.

1978 + First Races South of France

It was not long after I had regained the appetite for racing that the desire to race in a warmer climate manifested itself. Easter time, often a group of like-minded cotemporaries also raced in Provence, the extremely delightful area of Southern France. Often, Dale Coen travelled with Janet and me; he was a big help as a dog's body during the racing. We had a base in a campsite in the Presque Isle area near Toulon, hiring log cabin bungalows. This type of accommodation was new currently, since becoming more fashionable. Later, I was to learn that this campsite was badly affected by the forest fires that swept this area. The racing was for veterans only, had a very definite international flavour. Among our more serious competitors, we had the German Manfred Nepp, the Belgium Dauwalder, Pierre Aimar the Tour de France winner's brother. Among the British was Jack Wright, often my travelling companion, Brian Rourke, Jack Watson, Ben Thomas etc. All enjoying the southern ambience and the French way of life. The feel-good factor was a help in the good results we all had. Among the better results, was Jack first winning a stage in the Tour de Côte d'Azur, that finished at the summit of Mont Farron. I did the same the following year, having fooled the opposition two years running; the first year, I attacked arriving alone at the start of the Mont Farron climb. The opposition had to chase me while Jack sat on, of course, they caught me. For the following year, we did the same thing, excepting I had the better form. This time, the chasers failed to catch me; it was my turn for the win.

Another stage race I competed in, the last stage finished at a hotel and spar complex on the outskirts of St Tropez. This was owned and managed by a well-known French entertainment personality. Having to stay an extra day because of flight departure times, I had flown down alone; I realised this was the perfect place to run a training camp agreeing terms with the proprietor. The drawback turned out to be, there were no flights from the UK at the time I wanted to run the camp. Not deterred, a coach company was engaged to do the transport. Unfortunately, not enough bookings were forthcoming, we had to cancel. On the night all the riders left after the prize presentation, the hotel was extremely quiet. Going into the bar, I saw no other than Bridget Bardot and Elizabeth Taylor who sat in a secluded alcove having a cocktail. Bridget apparently was a friend of the proprietor, I received a courteous bonsoir Monsieur, that all, what a narrow escape.

Theo Kanel was the organiser of many of these veteran races in the early part of the year. He had rented a property in the area with his girlfriend for the winter. She also helped with the organisation, the two of them did a good job. Helping with the race marshalling on a corner, she had an error in her timing as we came round the corner; we caught her peeing in the middle of the road. This goes to show, that it was not only the French men who had these habits. Theo, when he was younger was employed as Chef de Service on board the cruise liner the Queen Elizabeth. He was noted as a good organiser, not so good it seems in organising his tax returns. In his native Switzerland where Theo ran a furniture business, they take very seriously the prompt declaration and payment of taxes. This tax situation was the explanation as to why he was out of commission for a while. It was Theo who arranged for several of us to compete in a race at Bormes-les-Mimosas on a Monday, 19 September 1988. This race was open to veterans and cyclo-sportives of all ages. Perhaps, the organisers thought that that these old veterans would be no match for the younger riders. They were wrong big time, as the Austrian with the unpronounceable name of Unter-Guggenberger disappeared up the road. In this criterium race, he was not to be seen again by the chasers until he crossed the finishing line. Jack and I led the chase after Unter unsuccessfully. For once, I beat Jack at the finish, making the result 1-2-3 for the foreigners. As the local newspaper reported it "une ecrasante Victoire des etrangers." As we had raced against Unter several times, we knew he was not this good. Later, he was absent from the races for a while, having been banned for doping. Theo himself was noted as a supercharger, having beaten the Pros in time trials on several occasions. Deuwalder was another one who on the face of it, did not win by natural means. In the first stage of the Tour de Mediterranean, he charged up the road from the start, coming a big cropper on the first roundabout, where the flowers had been watered. He picked himself up arriving at the finish, still alone and race leader. The picture of him in a *German Cycling* magazine, with his face all swollen at the finish, tells us something about his failure to feel all the pain.

Johan Bruyneel has a point, when he claims it is hypocrisy in denying Lance Armstrong his place among the biggest names. The super champions of the decade must have doped, because they would have been unable to beat the other champions, who had admitted to doping. Plenty of others would not agree with Johan, saying that in Armstrong's case, he was too professional at it One also must consider his scare when he contracted testicular cancer if what Sean Yates told me at the time is correct that "things did not look good at all for Lance as his cancer had spread throughout his body". This explains much as apparently Lance left no stone unturned in his quest to combat his illness. One would expect that this enhanced his knowledge of other products, at least his substantial work into the promotion of cancer charities should be acknowledged and taken into account. Tom Simpson paid for his errors with his life as did others.

In the case of Jacques Anquetil, it is significant that no one from his home area of Normandy, has not even promoted a cyclo-sportive in his honour. He was not a popular figure at all in his home area; no doubt, his well-documented relationship with the doctor and his wife, has not helped his cause. Doctors, especially sporting doctors, know all about drugs, it seems the late and great Jacques Anquetil is in the mind of many tarred with the same brush

Travel Agency Purchase and Business Expansion

My business affairs expanded quite significantly around 1984, with my selling the Garforth brokerage. This enabled me to buy a travel agency in Mexborough situated in the town centre next to the post office and 200 yards from my first brokerage. Also a further Halifax agency in Woodlands, another suburb of Doncaster. The seller of these businesses fortunately I knew very well over the years, although he was a competitor in the area where I lived, we had a good relationship, fortunately for me he was emigrating to New Zealand (he moved there because he thought it would be safer for his family in the case of a nuclear attack; as it turns out he is safer than us with the Covid pandemic). Originally, he wanted to sell the Woodlands business, which was a combined Halifax agency and travel agency to Les and Beryl, the travel agents in Garforth, who had been my co-tenants there. At the outset at this brokerage, where we shared the premises, they had used a clause in the lease enabling them to take over the whole floor, forcing me to move further up the high street. In the end, when I purchased the Woodlands Halifax agency along with the premises, Les and Beryl were left with just the travel agency they could purchase.

Understandably, they were not very pleased that I had purchased the Halifax Agency from under their noses, especially as they had given up their Garforth agency. They were even less pleased in years to come, when they learned my Mexborough travel agency which was purchased at the same time from the same vendor, as part of the same transaction, was doing much better than their travel agency was. Which gave me some satisfaction.

The Mexborough travel agency at this time had been open one year with a manager Dave Cook, on the owner's recommendation; I immediately made Dave a partner, changing the name to Ideal Travel. It was this name we put into the sponsorship of the Dinnington cycling club. As a result, we started to organise cycling training camps to Mallorca. Originally, the camps were in February and April; I did not want to step on Doug Petty's toes with his March camp. Before not very long, it was apparent that there was plenty of business to go round; anyway, my camps were at different locations, so we ran March camps as well.

Before not very long, I had acquired two more Halifax agencies in Tickhill and Harworth, the town where Tom was buried; both these businesses were run with different partners. The financial services headquarter were moved into the same building as the Halifax Agency in Edenthorpe which I now solely owned, where I had six registered independent financial advisers, plus support staff. Overall, I owned more than 50% of everything, plus one property and a 50% share in two others, I had overall control.

Training Camps in Mallorca

Our advantage in organising training camps was that we were fully-regulated travel agents, members of ABTA and ARTA. Consequently, we had access to the best deals in combined package holidays. During the winter months, many hotels at popular tourist destinations drastically reduced prices; some even operating at a loss in order to keep their staff employed. This is why in February; our camps were in Magaluf and Palma Nova. We also used the Taurus Park, a hotel down the bay from Palma towards the airport, almost in Arenal. We got to know the manager very well in this hotel. In addition, we had a couple of camps in Can Picafort, this location had the advantage of routes in all directions; regrettably, we only had good deals a couple of times, there were not the big hotels at this resort.

Initially, the Pollensa Park was only used in April, it was quite clear that as this was the preferred destination for many, we asked Pedro the manager to try opening in February for us to see if it was a success; of course it was, the Pollensa Park have never looked back since. In the beginning, the tour operators gave us one free place for every so many bookings. At the outset, this was quite generous; particularly, in Magaluf and Palma Nova, things however became gradually tighter as time went by. The big advantage in these discounts was that we were able to assist or give free places to individuals to act as runs leaders; don't forget we had the indefatigable Bill Cheadle a fixture as mechanic. Much time was spent at the airport as well as visiting hospitals and clinics all too frequently. Transferring bikes was not easy; to begin with, it is a piece of cake by comparison nowadays. Initially, there were only two firms authorised to transport the bikes, they really made a meal of it, charging waiting time at the airport without checking if the flight had been cancelled. In the winter, it was commonplace; despite this, they ignored our efforts to have them check flights out. As you can imagine, we were rather disgruntled not to put too fine a point on it, then we had the bright idea to hire buses to transport the bikes. This worked well the first year, the second year, things became very unpleasant, as the transport company workers blocked the road for the buses (a rather French habit). After that, the Balearics Authorities did not have much choice, but to give out more licences, if they wanted tourists.

Sometimes, Janet and I travelled from our holiday home, which we bought in 1990, in the Cotes de Goello, direct by car to Barcelona, where we took the ferry. One year, we arrived at the ferry embarkation office with our pre-booked tickets which included a cabin, to be told there weren't any cabins. I said, "They are reserved on the ticket"; they replied, "Your travel agent must have made a mistake."

"No," I retorted, "I am the travel agent, it was me that rang your office here, you gave me the reference numbers you see on the ticket, you had better go to see your boss to find me a cabin." An hour later, they found me a cabin, a nice one, it was with an outside window and free breakfast. On arrival, we had booked an apartment for several weeks, as we had clients arriving between the camps, we did this on four or five occasions.

At the outset, the February camp attracted the more serious riders, including the Percy Bilton team with Neil Martin (his son Dan is doing rather well now), Adrian Timmis, Steve Joughin. Paul Curran, John Walshaw. Mark Walsham, Steve, Bob and all, really enjoyed themselves mixing with everyone. Some of their training was spent even riding with other guests; good for them, this was well appreciated. We also had the Raleigh team; they mostly did their own thing. February was initially our busiest time but when the National Lottery put money into British Cycling, they paid for many of the rider's jaunts, officials too. This meant for us, April gradually became our busiest time.

Training Camp Continue Finding Your Way

We had many other riders apart from Nev, who liked to find their way on their own; among them were two senior riders Eileen and Bill, they did not find it easy to find their way about. Accurate maps for the back roads did not exist. Max Huerzelers Swiss group produced their own, their riders were mostly German whose numbers dwarfed ours, even though at that time, we were the largest group from the UK. They had set routes on their maps, as we wanted quieter roads, we avoided their routes as much as possible. Nowadays, if you want quieter roads, the best chance is to go on some of the Camino's, but that is not guaranteed; no doubt things have changed with coronavirus.

Anyway, Eileen and Bill had heard that some military survey maps were available in Pollensa town. Our hotel was at Cala Bona at that time, so they had some kilometres to put in. Eileen told Bill to stay strictly on her wheel when they arrived at Pollensa. This was a good plan as in the restaurant when she sent him for her second helpings, he had trouble finding his way back to the table; it helped if he followed the floor lights. Of course, we stayed in some swish places most of the time. Disaster struck on their arrival at Pollensa, looking behind, Bill was not in sight, riding round for some time, she was unable to find him. Next was a trip to the local police station to see if he had been in an accident, where there were no reports of anything untoward. The police chief could see she was upset, asking if they were married; the answer was NO, then it does not matter he said matter of fact. "Ah, it does was the reply; he has the money."

"Then we had better look for him," was the answer. The motor cyclist despatched eventually finding him, tapped him on the shoulder, telling him, "We have your wife in the police station."

"Why? What has she done wrong?" was the reply. Arriving for the usual evening meeting innocent looking, but late, Eileen told me what had happened, saying we did not want to be late for the meeting, so we shared the shower. These meetings were an important feature as we discussed the next day's ride, inevitable someone always asked where the coffee stop was, more importantly, how they would find the bar, the answer was always the same, in the square next to the church. Sometimes, we had a question-and-answer meeting; the answers with Sean Yates were very illuminating. Then we had Bill Cheadle give a lecture on how to look after your bike, sorry only joking. Another time, we had a discussion on whether it was a good idea to wear a helmet, or not. This was when we had been to the Monastery at San Salvador. I had instructed my group to regroup for the return, at the junction at the bottom of this dangerous decent. At the junction, one rider was missing, waiting for a while as he had not appeared, we started to look for him. At the very last bend, it was myself that heard a feeble groan; he had overshot the last bend, ending up part way up a dirt path bleeding with his head cut.

Luckily, there was a Red Cross aid station nearby; they had a lot of work with cyclists crashing on the descent, they did well to fix him up, having plenty of experience, but apparently not for brain injuries. Next day, he arrived at the meeting to take part in this discussion with his face swollen and head bandaged, on the vote as to wearing helmets to everyone's amazement, he was against the idea. He was a cycle dealer in the south; obviously, he did not want to sell helmets, I thought the head damage was more than you could see.

After a visit to the aforesaid monastery, two young ladies were very impressed with Timoner's world motor paced world championship jerseys, but could not understand how their feet had overheated in the coffee shop. "Did you sit at a table with a very long cloth almost touching the ground?" I asked. "YES," was the reply. "That explains it." I told them, "There was a charcoal tray burning under the table, it is a tradition since the monks used this room as a dining room." Of course, everyone knew of Guillermon Timoner's-six world championship motor paced gold medals plus two silvers, having seen his jerseys in the monastery, what many did not know, was that he still had a bike shop in Felanitx, the next town to the monastery. One day, Dave Marsh and myself arranged with his daughter who ran the shop to meet Guillermon, Dave having professed that he wanted to ride motor paced and learn more about the equipment.

Guillermon showed us his cane wheels, enormous chain rings, the whole caboodle, which looked even more amazing because Timoner was only a small guy. Luckily for us, he was very charming, taking great delight in explaining things to us with a great insight into the intriguing motor paced world, an unforgettable experience for our part. If Dave really wanted to know more about modern equipment, he could do no better than visit me in my Brittany Village of Plouha where I could introduce him to Daniel Salmon, who had his workshop and retail shop nearby. Daniel was a world amateur motor paced medal winner, he did build equipment for the French national team; at a time when frames were hand built to your personal requirements, he was noted for setting you up with the right position on your bike for your particular skills. Latterly he could repair carbon frames when no one else was doing this, he was known in the UK for the Salmon mudguards, the strong narrow ones that were hardly affected with the wind.

Another real speed merchant was Fred Rompelberg, who I got to know in the early days at the Taurus Park. He set a world absolute speed record, on a bike of course in 1995, of 268 km/hour on the salt flats of Salt Lake City. When I first made his acquaintance, he was just setting up his touring business after a spell with Max Hurzeiler; like many, he was having trouble with his bike transfers; fortunately, we were able to help him out. Another one who we were able to rescue with the same problem was Colin Lewis, his clients came to us the following year; a year on, we were pleased to see him back in business. Joining the illustrious list, or infamous list depending on your point of view, was Johan Bruyneel who used to have a beer with me and others from our group in the local bar near the Taurus Park; who would have thought that this nice friendly guy was to become so controversial in the Lance Armstrong affair. At that time, he was in the Spanish Once team doing his own training for the Grand Prix de Nations time trial, which for some reason was held in Mallorca in 1992; he beat Tony Rominger by five seconds.

Advice was forthcoming at different times from John Herety, Phil Thomas, Steve Joughin, PhGriffiths, Sean Yates, Peter Longbottom, John Tanner, Sid Barras, Kevin Dawson, Paul Curran, Adrian Timmis, which is not a complete list in no particular order. One of the things that was stressed at the first meeting, especially for those doing two weeks, was the importance of pacing yourself; it was noticeable towards the end of the two weeks that the numbers on the organised runs dwindled, understandably natural enthusiasm in the beginning having an effect. Attention was paid to the weather in choosing the runs, especially on the earlier camps; we insisted that if it was wet, not to do the mountains as it was too dangerous, especially the tunnel at the top of Puig Meyor on the route to Soller. Even in the dry in the early days, this tunnel was lethal, it was dark and wet with pot holes. The one just as you were coming out of the tunnel was easily the worst; on one occasion I hit the hole coming out sideways, sliding into the parking space with two flat tyres to join numerous others mending punctures. Fortunately, for me, Jack Wright who I was riding with was also riding tubulars, so we were ok. As the numbers riding tubulars became less and less, I switched to tyres the next trip.

It was Wooley Jumper who ignored the advice not to do the Puig Meyer ride in the wet, he had flu like symptoms afterwards, this ruining his entire racing season. The Wooley Jumper that he always wore, hence the nickname, obviously was not effective. Even the manager of the Taurus Park, Manual Martinez, who was himself a bike rider, told me he had once been caught out with the weather on this ride; his hands had become so cold he was compelled to search for plastic bags thrown in the waste bins for protection.

Mallorca training camp Hatters bike in the sea and dead dogs

A very unpleasant sight that we came across all too often on our rides were dead dogs at the side of the road, with the warmer climate, these easily swelled to a good size; indeed, you could easily think they were dead pigs with their feet starkly pointed skywards. I am claiming the credit for solving this problem, it happened like this; Pedro Canalles the owner of the San Diego and Solimar Hotels was the president of the Mallorca Cycling Federation; I knew him well from the stays in his hotels during the veterans Tour of Mallorca, Doug Petty also worked with him. He proposed me to the Mallorca Government to receive an award for helping to bring tourism to the island. On the appointed day, I along with Pedro and some of his clubmates from Arenal went to the governor's magnificent palace in Palma. As you would expect, we only drank the best champagne and I was presented with an inscribed plaque plus a racing jersey designed by a Mallorca artist, the same jersey as Ken Cowdell was presented with for his stage win in the Tour of Mallorca. This was presented not by the mere governor of Mallorca but by the governor of the Balearic Islands, nonetheless. He was to ask me if there was anything that could be done to help tourism, I replied, "Yes, get rid of the sight of dead dogs that lay around for several days, even weeks." The reply was, "It's not possible; there are no dead dogs left on our roads." A chorus of voices immediately intervened saying, "Yes, there is." AFTER THAT, NO DEAD DOGS.

Training Camps Mallorca Bill Cheadle, Personalities and Nicknames

Many riders hid nicknames; usually, Pete Mathews was the main instigator. Even his own son, Lea had the nickname laptop (small pc); others were Captain Cruelty, Wooley Jumper, Mad Hatter, Griffo, Pedalling Crank, his son, Odd Crank. Many are self-explanatory; there were many others. We covered perhaps every road on the island overall, with different camps, mountains, hilly, fiat all the spectrum, varying speeds, long runs, shorter ones, some with one stop, others with many for the more serious, no stops. Essential to this was our excellent run leaders of various calibres and many talents, not all on the bike. Top of the range, the most capable of riders in all circumstances was Sean Yates, Tour de France yellow jersey, an entertaining informative personality with many stories to tell Neil Martin, a professional who had twice competed in the Olympics; the father of the current top professional Dan Martin, who rides for Ireland. His mother is the sister of Stephen Roche; Dan was born in England. Neil was a member of my own club, the

Dinnington, a nicer person and gentleman you could not expect to meet.

A key member of the team was the evergreen Ken Cowdel, Captain Cruelty to his friends. He knew the roads like the back of his hand, also knowing the Cami camino's (tracks) that had been tarmacked that no one else knew. He was indefatigable; always the most obliging of helpers. One day, we had a bit of sprint up the long drag from Montuiri to Randi. Someone switched. Ken and the Culprit went over the edge of the road down the slope on the right. We pulled him back up the steep slope by his feet; he had hurt himself a little, another rider had punctured in this crash. Ken pumped his tyre up blood and sweat dripping in the road. My business partner at Ideal Travel, Dave Cook took out a steadier group, he was a worrier-always concerned that everybody was enjoying themselves. Consequently, he was taken advantage of, left to sit on the front all day.

Don Turner was another who took out a steady group, he was a retired bank manager from Blackpool who knew everybody from that part of the world. Then, we had Sammy Shear a larger-than-life character, although he was small; he had moved permanently to Porto Pollensa. If you described him as a camp follower, no one would depute this he knew all the best restaurants, so you would never go hungry. Pete Mathews could be relied on to be entertaining but not to find his way. He had been going to Mallorca for years; like any sprinter, he preferred to follow wheels; he thought we were unaware. Also, it was necessary to understand run leaders' dialects, the best-known phrase was that of the Dinnington Club's secretary Joe Marsh, 'watch out for oils a Oses' which translates to pot holes and horses. In reality, there were plenty of pot holes in the beginning but not many horses; Joe remembered an entanglement with a horse when he was younger. Myself, when we were traversing the Albufeira marsh road probably breached racial guidelines in sometimes asking riders to watch out for the Panza Division and Parachutists.

Big Germans on heavy Dutch bikes with packs on their backs; if you wanted to talk football; you rode with Neil Nel Higgins. He was a Preston North End supporter; I don't know why when you heard him say 'come on riders,' it was the kick off. Jim Macarthy from Scotland was a very conscientious leader, crossing the sometimes-busy main road from Boger to Campanet, he paid more attention to everyone else, falling off himself, luckily without damage.

Among the leaders, we had our friend from back home in South Yorkshire, Kattie Allen, together with Maxine Johnson, many of the younger riders wanted to ride behind Kattie when she wore her gold-coloured shorts. Much of Maxine's training was done following her husband's wheel. Keith the husband was ever present, not giving the youngster's much of a chance to ride with her alone. Peter Longbottom was a helper before he was tragically killed in a road accident while riding to meet his local chain gang one evening. What a loss.

Two other helpers we had one year were Sid Barras and Doug Dailey among others, thanks to them all. Among our many guests was Nev Chanin, the one million mile plus tourist, sometimes he rode with a group but was much more at home riding alone; he said he was delighted to have discovered Mallorca on our camps, it was much better in the winter than riding in the wilds of Patagonia. One of his touring secrets I learned was in order to keep his cycle weight down, he posted clothing to various post offices on route, returning the dirty ones by the same method.

Last but not the least, being the most important member of our team was our mechanic Bill Cheadle, nothing was too much trouble for Bill; his knowledge and skill was second to none. He had an important role to play as a British cycling mechanic often at the Manchester track. What is not known to everyone is that he was exceptionally generous, giving what help he could to youngsters. At one period, he had trouble with the customs and excise control at Dover when he had been to Belgium buying large amount of cycling clothing, which he gave free of charge to deserving youngsters. Eventually, after some time, he became fed up with this constant harassment, challenging the customs as to what was going on, it transpired that he was on a list, apparently having been reported for bringing large amounts of clothing into the country without paying taxes. It transpires that it was a local cycle dealer who had signalled this, as they considered they were losing out on significant clothing sales to the youngsters. I am sorry to say that this was in stark contrast to our star local rider Tom,(Simpson) who had a habit of selling tatty trade clothing to the youngsters at a ridiculous price, whenever he came home, I had personally asked him to be more reasonable.

Bill who drove a fuel tanker for a living, became famous one day in this respect, he was famous otherwise, his big tanker broke down right on the hole in the ground roundabout in the centre of Sheffield, causing a grid block in the city and environs for the whole of the day. After this episode, I think it is fair to say, Bill was the instigator for the substantial road works in the city, that later took place. He related to me that occasionally he had to sit in with prospective tanker driver applicants, to see how they performed behind the wheel. He had one who grumbled about cyclists, needless to say he did not succeed with his application. Being a camp mechanic had its bad moments, particularly at the very big hotels, deaths were not unknown among the guests, the mechanic who was more often than not placed near the back entrance to the hotel, had to witness the dead bodies being quietly exited.

Training Camp Continued
The Good, the Bad and the Ugly

It was Manual, the manager of the Taurus Park, himself a cyclist, who was to save Wayne Randel maybe from a night with the Policia; *ignorance is bliss* in Wayne's case. On this camp, our arrangements with this hotel were with Thompsons, the tour operator for a complete package, flight, transport to the hotel excluding the bikes, with half board. The tour operator was also selling through their normal channels, not with us, direct flights only, full stop, nothing else, no transport, no hotel, nothing; you made your own arrangements on arrival. As was normal, our guests arrived at different times, as we had flights from all over the UK. On the night in question, I was having a drink with Jack as was often the case in the bar down the road, when Tony Holmes a frequent guest, came into the bar complaining that Wayne Randel was in his place, in his room. Tony was fixed up with another room, the management issued messages on the hotel loudspeaker system for Wayne to contact the reception, together with notes pushed under the door of his new found accommodation. Wayne ignored these messages for a couple of days, despite being visible to all and sundry; he was certainly having the breakfasts at least. Finally, with no result after a couple of days, Manual himself came out to the front of the hotel, where we were assembling for the ride, asking Dave Cook to point out Snr Randel; having no option, he did. Wayne was marched back into the hotel, a little while later, Wayne was cow-tailing it down the road, doing a balancing act with his suitcase on his handlebars to an enormous cheer.

Incidents that you could manage without were extremely rare, cyclists by enlarge are reasonable people. We had an old track cyclist from Sheffield, the last time he raced I think, it was on a Dursley Pederson; he was in such a poor state of health, I thought it prudent to warn the tour operators representative that we had a client who I thought, would probably have to be repatriated. The Rep replied "A**h, we spotted him at the airport, it not so unusual**."

"It is on a cycle training camp," I replied.

On another occasion, this time at the Puerto Azul Hotel in Porto Pollensa, we had a CTTC (The touring organisation) rider who must have been in his 90s, arrived quite legitimately with two 70-80-year-old females in cycling outfits with their crash helmet still perched on their heads; according to the tour operators' personnel, they arrived like this at the airport on their bikes. Their bikes were transported intact on the plane, where they sat in their seats with their crash hats still on. For the return, I tried to communicate with them as to the time their bus left, to no avail, despite leaving messages in their room. When they came out of their room, the allocated bus had long gone to the airport, they boarded another bus immediately, no waiting about like the rest of us, then straight on to the plane, no problem, unbelievable. Next year, Dave informed me that they had booked again, when I told Dave to send their money back, the reply was, "I cannot do that."

"You had better do it," was my response and he did.

Initially, very few people hired bikes, some had proper bike boxes, others had bags or a special way of packing their own bike. The honour of having the largest package fell to Clive, a lorry driver by trade, which perhaps explains how he transported it to the airport. He used to come with a tandem; he rode with his wife, plus a solo bike for himself. Somehow, he had at least one wooden box to protect his equipment, telling everyone that he was not happy with his design, but for next year, he would improve on it with a bigger box. Keeping his promise, the following year, on arriving with the box everyone came to marvel at him unpack two bikes, after the task was done, he said, "I do not know what to do with the box." Some wag at the back said, "**PUT THE HOTEL IN IT.**"

A climb that was not my favourite was the Calobra although I enjoyed the spectacular walk through the tunnel at the bottom. A couple of lady riders remarked that they liked going down the snake like decent but not the toil back up, a view that I had much sympathy with. For the following year I devised a plan where we would descend the Calobra then for the return a boat would take us back to Pollensa Port, it was not too expensive but not enough people were willing to splash out, so the boat trip sank. However, on one run the sea was to play its part in the proceedings, this particular day we had a run to Porto Christo near the caves of Drac, on arrival at the promenade this time, the bikes were parked on the railings. Suddenly there was a big gust of wind resulting in one bike finishing in the sea out of sight, it had to be the

Hatters bike. Fortunately, there was a Tri-athlete with the group, without hesitation he dived in to try to recover the bike, without success to start with. What saved the day at least for Dereck, (I think the day was made for the others) was his streamlining theory of the moment, he had the small Cinnelli tri-bar extensions that were later banned for racing, to these Dereck had wrapped some of his belongings in a bright red plastic bag in the form of a ball, like you see on the prow of a ship. Maybe this was where he had retrieved the idea, one can only surmise as it was impossible to fathom out how the Hatter brain functioned. It was the bright red ball that caught the intrepid eye of our diver, enabling him to recuperate the bike. On the way back to the Hotel Dereck was to remark that his bike had never run better, this I do not doubt.

Sorrento Training Camp

Ideal Travel organised one other training camp other than Mallorca; this was in Sorrento, Italy in April. The year previous to the camp, I flew to Naples staying in Sorrento for four nights to see if it was viable, of course I took my bike. On arrival, the first day I was keen to get out on my bike, setting off to sample the piece de resistance of the rides from Sorrento, the garden route known throughout the world, the hard route round the coast with short sharp climbs with many spectacular twists and turns looking vertiginously down at the sea. Soon, I was passed by small groups of riders in what apparently was a race; not wanting to interfere, I did not jump on to anyone's wheel to start with, when several groups had passed, I could not resist any longer jumping at the back of a group without problem. I am not saying it was easy but I was coping well enough. After several kilometres, passing groups of spectators, a shining new convertible with a commissaire aboard I assumed, pulled alongside, I took him to say I should not be there, which I knew full well, I replied I am out training and they were not going very quick as to him understanding or not, I knew not, with that he disappeared, I heard no more.

I continued through a couple more villages with buntings flapping in the breeze in tune with the cheering crowds before I desisted. After this exhilarating ride and unforeseen turn of events on returning to the hotel, I was gob smacked to learn that it was the Tirranno Adriaticco that I had just witnessed not long after the start of the first stage in Naples, having not done many kilometres before they caught me; I can only assume that at that time, most of the riders had not specially prepared for the race, but were using it as a training event.

The following year, the camp was for two weeks in a smallish hotel that was reasonably comfortable with food served at the table. On the runs, it became more apparent that there was more rain than in Mallorca, just as I had witnessed the previous year. Everyone thought the garden route was as magnificent as claimed but no better than the Tramuntana routes in Mallorca; perhaps, a little harder as we needed two more sprockets on a couple of steeper climbs that finished at ski stations. Because of the rain one day, we cut short the garden route circuit by turning earlier than planned off the coast road going through a pass in the mountains towards Naples. When it rained again, I managed to sniff out a good local restaurant in the next village having a nose for finding them, the meal was the standard meal of the day with the red wine included, which tasted like Tizer; it was agreeable enough drinking plenty, we were quite happy despite the continuing rain. Perhaps, in this what seemed like a lost valley, the wine tasing like Tizer was the norm, vintage Tizer! A new appellation perhaps?

Now, the riders from South Yorkshire know what Tizer tastes like, or used to, not anybody else; so, I will explain that there is a mineral water manufacturer that makes soft drinks. Tizer is or was their speciality, a point of interest is that it was owned by the parents of a certain William Haigh who was to become home secretary under Margaret Thatcher. His drinking habits came under scrutiny much later in an interview with the BBC; he had claimed that as a youngster, he regularly drank l0 to 15 pints of beer a night with the local furnace fettlers; this seemed a little farfetched, but it was not. I can tell you that on leaving school, as I explained earlier, working at British Steel, I became familiar with the conditions that the furnace fettlers worked in, they need to take in a lot of liquid to replace that lost in the extreme heat of the furnace when they had to fettle it, so the young William was in this sort of company in his local bar, from what one hears drinking habits in Parliament are not much better.

Back to Sorrento which certainly is a super holiday destination with plenty to see; Pompei, Herculean, Positano, Amalfi, Naples, Vesuvius, Capri; the list goes on. We certainly profited in the sightseeing having more rest days than usual because of the rain. I can add that I have never seen as many different types of bars and coffee shops as I saw in Sorrento until I went to live in the East Algarve, Portugal in the winter. Saturday at the hotel along with the staff and a full complement of waiters, we were all watching the Milan-San Remo classic, the Italian star Moreno Argentin broke away on the climb being alone at the summit of this last climb with the descent down to the finish to the adoration of the cheering delirious Italians in the room. This joy was short lived as he was joined on the descent by no other than Sean Kelly; in the sprint finish there was only going to be one possible outcome, we looked around, all the Italians had disappeared into thin air.

Names for Places

Back to Mallorca for the next camp, although Sorento was a worthwhile trip being an experience and good sightseeing destination. In the opinion of most, Mallorca was not to be beaten. Mallorca was now part of our lives; we even had our own nicknames for many places and routes. Ken's Conk for the steep twisting little brute of a hill between Sant Llorenc and the Arta Petra Road. Dead Legs Gulch was the appropriately named route on leaving Alaro, between the huge pillars of rock, popular with climbers, the even crazier variety, up over the Orient climb to Bunyola. Shindlers Gap was the Camino through the woods towards Sa Pobla, not forgetting when returning to Puerto Pollensa, it was either by the Bumps or through the Marshes.

There was a nasty hole on the descent just before arriving at Cala Bona which caused several riders to puncture; one was Lennie Benton who complained bitterly about it, he did not complain so virulently about puncturing in a race; even Sean Yates was a victim of this same hole. Finally, Sean on the next run on this route went equipped with some white paint and a brush arriving at the hole first, not difficult for him, he painted a big white circle round the hole. Thereafter, for quite some time, it was known as Lennie's hole.

Ken and myself found a short cut on the road from Son Carrio to avoid going into Manacor, when taking the road which went up Ken's Conk, there you go! I do not know another way to describe the route. When we found the short cut, the road looked as if it was only going to a farm on a bend, after 10 yards, there was a left turn at the side of a big gate to someone's house, this was a road. We kept this secret as long as we could; some thought we had break away qualities that we did not possess. When in Arenal, we took the back road to Llucmajor to avoid the busier direct road, which was a bit like riding up a series of steps, this was before the new motorway type road was built. On the way back, our instructions were not to continue all the way to Palma, instead turn left on seeing the sign for Arenal. We had one Dinnington non-racing member, who nevertheless arrived in Palma, setting off back wrongly up the real motorway; in his confusion which got worse, he went down someone's drive knocking on the door to ask the way. As fate would have it, they gave him a tomato sandwich and brought him back to the hotel; they turned out to be from Rotherham. The record for the longest return by taxi falls to my friend Jack and his son Michael; they were caught in a fierce thunderstorm near Palma, the water was so deep that the young Michael refused to ride any further, only Jack could have afforded the fare back to Puerto Pollensa.

When we had the February camps in Magaluf, we knew a way via Calvia to avoid going through Palma as the city was very busy, even in winter. This route was rarely used as it was rather hard to find; it also went near a military firing area. Consequently, we were wary of shells whistling over our heads. The necessity to go through Palma meant that when we were able to find other destinations, Magaluf was dropped.

Stephen Roach organised his training camps, in a hotel which I believe he owned, which was on the wrong side of Palma in my opinion. I read latterly in the press that he was having financial difficulties with this enterprise; I think he was in the wrong place, with the passage of time the traffic became even heavier Nevertheless, he kept going for much longer than us, but of course if you run up massive debts then you can although at the time his brother-in-law Neil Martin preferred to be with us, where he was very much appreciated. I did hear on the grapevine from reliable sources, that at the time, he did his fabulous triple, he was rather difficult to get on with, he was on cloud nine, who would not be with this achievement. Apparently, this episode I have reason to believe was completely out of character, as everyone involve with him since say how pleasant and gentlemanly, he is. Certainly, the people who meet him among the 10,000 riders at the Pierre Le Bigault cyclo-event at Callac in Brittany, have nothing but the highest praise for his deportment. This is no longer the case in Mallorca where he now dares not set foot.

Wherever we have been staying on the island, we have always found our way to Gomela's bike shop. From a modest start in Palma, we have seen it grow into the modern emporium of today in Binnisalem. Another popular visit in this town that has always **gone down well**, *it would*, was the visit to the Bodega for wine tasting with a meal.

Hazards and Accidents

One other activity undertaken by a few was racing in the local races at Arenal, organised by the local club. I was due to ride once, having a bad cold, I went to watch instead, seeing three or four different finishing lines, I did not know which one was in use. This finishing area was at the industrial site at the Headland towards Cap Blanc, nobody knew which line was the correct one, along with others, we waited. Finally, we saw the flashing lights of the lead vehicles arriving, then we saw several flashing lights, resulting in three different finishes, three different riders all thought they had won the race. That was it; I gave up any thoughts of riding events in the future. We have seen flashes of this disorganisation in the Tour of Mallorca, which I write about later.

Another race was run by Trevor Maddens group; this was a two up time trial. Against my better judgement, Lennie Benton talked me into riding this with him. The first leg was down the bay to the first island at Alcudia, Lennie had me absolutely hung on by the skin of my teeth. The next leg was over the humps to the Island at Pollensa town when I did the same thing to Lennie, that was it; never again. Ideal Travel did some of the travel arrangements for Trevor Maddens group and Ken Cowdell was a run leader for a time. However, we were not involved in the apartment bookings with the Pollensa Park, in which they had problems with the then trusted treasurer Stan Turner.

The meals in the hotels were always buffet style, including the breakfast, making it easy to take food out for the back pocked later in the day. The management was always aware of this. In the Pollensa Park, they had a very keen Ayatollah who kept a close eye on things. It was Jebb, always a joker, who decided to test him out. Amusing himself and everybody, he took a complete bunch of bananas over his shoulder, almost too heavy to carry; then tried to nonchalantly stroll outside. It backfired on him, as thereafter if he had been in Alcaraz, he could not have been more closely watched.

Occasionally, a few of us ate a restaurant meal at lunchtime, usually under the instigation of Sammie who lived alone, so you can understand why. Bill Cheadle for a long time would eat only English food. After the passage of time, a long time, we finally re-educated him a little; he started to appreciate the food at Tollo's Bar. Kattie, Ken and myself when we were in Magaluf, ate in a restaurant at Calvia belonging to an ex-pro, a team mate of Jan Ulrich; he was very professional and charming, letting us sit in the place normally reserved for Jan. His food would even gain praise from Sammie. After a long French style meal, we gingerly negotiated the long descent back to Magaluf, Kattie was in a better state than we were, even though she had outclassed us in the drinking stakes. Meeting others from the group when we returned, no one wanted to linger talking to us; we later learned it was because we stank of garlic. Kattie perhaps would not have the success with the two husbands she met on the camp, if that had been her regular perfume. Did I say success, yes with number two, but according to husband number one's mother and father, Laptop blew a fuse, which was no fault of Kattie. For good Mallorca food, the Cellar restaurants can normally be recommended. For a reasonably price meal of the day, there are restaurants throughout the island; if you look carefully where the locals are eating, there is a very good one with a French cook near the Roman bridge in Pollensa town.

Riding a bike as we know is hazardous, very occasionally, but all too often leading to accidents and misfortunes. I believe with care, our run leaders kept this to a minimum, I am not aware of anyone with lasting damage. Nonetheless, Dave, myself and Janet, my first wife must have visited just about every clinic and hospital on the island at some time or the other. The best one to visit, from a visitor's point of view, was the private clinic in Palma, specialising in bone fractures, having a very pleasant cafeteria, overlooking the millionaire's yachts in the harbour.

It was on a very long fast descent, on the coast road from Andraix towards Solar, when one rider did not take the bend. There were four of us in line trying to re-join the Percy Bilton Pros after being dropped on a climb, when this happened. I was last in the line, seeing the third rider horrifyingly disappear over the edge of the road. On looking down, there was a sheer drop and the rider, the Percy Bilton Mechanic, was lying face down on the only tiny flat piece of ground, besides a massive rock just like the stone blocks the pyramids were built with, surrounded by all sorts of smaller rocks and rubbish; I though he must be dead. Climbing down to him, we could see he was still breathing, but in some pain; the debris all around him was the result of previous accidents, where vehicles had not negotiated the bend. Later, we were to learn three people had been killed previously in one wreck we saw. When the ambulance arrived, the crew refused to descend to carry him back to the road; we managed it, cycling shoes notwithstanding. The worst injury was to his leg, he was back in the hotel after three days in the hospital; back home, he was soon riding his bike again. I am pleased to say very conspicuous warning signs are now in place on this bend.

Sammie was another who had a bad accident while riding with friends, a couple of whom were from our camp. He hit a dog full on, shearing his forks clean off, landing very heavily on his head; the dog disappeared. Sammie was ambulanced urgently to the Muro Private Hospital, where he was between life and death for a couple of days. Close friends of his, Phil Griffiths and Tollo were close to tears after visiting him, seeing what state he was in. Sammie who wanted his bike to be as light as possible had fitted the carbon head piece to the top of the forks, against the advice of Phil at the time. Janet and myself had a Siamese cat 10 years old, left behind in the cattery during our absence; our cat was named Sammie after the aforesaid, you do not need any imagination as to why if you know anything about Siamese cats. Unbelievably, you could not make this up, we received a telephone call from the cattery the night of the accident, the cat had been found dead; apparently, with a heart attack.

Another accident-prone place was the halt sign at the junction between Sa Pobla and the entrance to the track on the waterpipe road to Santa Maria. On the right of the halt sign was a deep ditch that should have been filled in; this is Spain, don't forget. On several occasions, there was a minor mishap at this junction caused by a lack of attention; we have had riders hanging like a trapeze artist from the cabling to avoid dropping in the ditch. Another time after just crossing the junction, four or five of us had to swerve into the bushes on the right. We quickly continued on our route; then one rider who had crashed into the bushes discovered he had lost his wallet. Going back, after a search, it was recovered along with quite a collection of sunglasses, obviously the same thing had frequently happened to others at the same spot.

Repairs to machines can sometimes be achieved in the most unlikely manor, near Algadia, my seat pin bolt sheared off abruptly with a loud crack; I suppose it was metal fatigue; it is very uncomfortable riding a long way without a seat pin. Dave Marsh's ingenuity in spotting a child's bike in a rubbish bin saved the day, when the seat pin bolt he had extracted fitted. Accidents can have their funny side, but not always to the person concerned, being with a group repairing a puncture on the crossroads, where the rapid descent down the mountain from Valdamosa, turns left to Bunyola, when the really serious group with Tanner, Longbottom, Curran etc., came hurling down at great speed in single file. Last in the group was Wayne Randall trying to get back on a wheel; he did not make the corner, disappearing in a big cloud of dust. Shaking off the dust like a dog does, he was back on his bike again in a flash, chasing after them to a bigger cheer than if we had won the world cup again. Wayne Randall is from Barnsley; they are tough from Barnsley. It seems out of character that people from this part of the world address one another as flower, petal, love, ducky, but they do. Another rider from Barnsley, this time a lady, lost it on the descent from Cura towards Montuiri. Fortunately, she was tough, as her excursion over the terrain was arrested with a painful embrace of a man-sized CATI. The Mad Hatter had an interesting week removing all the needles back at the hotel.

For many years, we did not have trouble with the insurance picking up the hospital bills, including the private hospitals following accidents and illnesses. Things started to change when Lennie Grayson crashed and was taken to the private hospital in Muro. The insurers were mostly controlled by a central bureau, who acted for several insurers. They started to have the idea that the private hospitals were too expensive for various reasons, as opposed to the public hospitals. They wanted to direct clients to public hospitals in the first place. As in the case of Lennie, they moved him from the private domain to the public, despite protests that they waited until later, when it was safe to do so, not move him in the middle of the night. Lennie had a head injury, despite much time spent on the telephone with the insurance bureau, I got nowhere; despite my going to the hospital in the middle of the night, I was still unable to pursued them that this was not in the client's interest. In due course, Lennie recovered, we next met when we were both riding a local race; he was ok, but his wife was rather hostile to me, thinking I was not very sympathetic at the time of the accident. It appears that when trying to reassure her by saying, you have been there when he has crashed in a race, it is no worse or different, she took it the wrong way; sorry failed again; perhaps, I should have handled it differently.

The roads have gradually improved since the beginning of our camps, especially those used by cyclists were often in a dreadful state, the caves road being the worst. Can Picafort where your wheel could drop in a rain drain cover was very dangerous; there were many more. This really was inexcusable, bearing in mind the amount of money cyclists brought to the island at the quieter times. Now, thankfully the message has largely been received; the roads are substantially better than they were. Many of the previously unused Camino tracks have been tarmacked, the improvement in the cave's road is very noticeable, now with signs giving cyclists priority.

Not all the lessons have been learned. I am talking about cycle paths. For many years, the cycle path at the edge of the Albufeira marsh from Alcudia to Can-Picafort was lethal. It took many complaints, including at least two deaths, for this to be resolved. The mostly German-speaking cyclists from the Alcudia area were the main instigators of this change, organising at least two sit-ins blocking the road. Now, a track at each side of the road has been constructed despite the restrictions of the Albufeira marsh; this is a big improvement.

Despite this history, the lessons have not been learned by everyone, perhaps due to fragmented governance. Regrettably, a new track was built only at the sea side between Puerto Pollensa and Alcudia, with two-way traffic, this is far too dangerous, not fit for purpose. Slower tourist riders are the ones taking the track from the holiday complex into Alcudia, adding to the danger. It is all too easy to be pushed into the path of the motorised traffic with disastrous consequences. It is hard to understand why with the history of the Albufeira path that the cycle path was not constructed at each side of the road. Many of us ride down the bay to Alcudia, avoiding coming back the same way. There is an alternative road that goes a little inland, and it is not too hard to find, not much further and quite pleasant.

Two years ago, I was on a visit in April setting off to ride down the bay alone to Alcudia when a large group appeared, coming from the promenade at Puerto Pollensa and setting off to ride down the cycle path. I shouted to them it is best at my side of the road, in reply a lady in a very loud voice enquired why. Despite my saying, it was dangerous on their side, this advice was ignored, as they carried on. About ten minutes later, arriving in the vicinity of the holiday camp, there was a rider sprawled out on the road, who had crashed on the cycle path, being tended by his friends. I was later to learn it was another fatality, which must have been witnessed by the group I shouted to.

My Retirement from Ideal Travel Continued from Hazards and Accident

After many years, almost twenty, of organising the training camps, it became more difficult, almost impossible to obtain discounts from the tour operators. For Dave, the difficulty of earning enough to pay helpers to run the groups in a professional manner, was an important factor. Following the accident that our former club member Alan Geldard was sued for, while helping Trevor Maddens club group, this rather unnerved Dave from doing any further organisation. For him, it was too much work for little reward; I suspect that Dave's new wife had an influence in this. For me, insurance was the obvious answer, as a former broker working with Lloyds of London, I can tell you this was not a viable proposition at that time. There were other solutions, such as forming a separate company to run the groups. My suggestion that we should organise differently, even organising something in East Algarve, where I was going to live in the winter, did not appeal to Dave. This was a big opportunity missed; there is still a tremendous opportunity to run groups from this location. This being more important to Dave and our clients than to me personally, as I was now passed retirement age.

When you look at the substantial increase in cycling traffic to Mallorca, one wonders what we were thinking of. At the last count before the pandemic, one person had 600 clients in Mallorca, despite my hearing there was a very substantial number of complaints as to the organisation, the same person had 1200 clients the following year, kick yourself, Dave. Whilst I was willing to continue by obtaining a new manager in place of Dave, I gave Dave the option of him or me taking over the travel agency 100%. It appears to have been touch and go before Dave finally decided it would be him.

Seniors Having Fun

Tour of Luxembourg

I rode the veterans Tour of Luxembourg seven times to be exact the "Ronde de Luxembourg, Fete du Raisin et du Vin." Often, I was accompanied by my pal and clubmate, Dale Coen who did sterling work as a driver and being a great help with the race affairs. In my opinion, this 5-day stage race which had been held continually since 1946, was the best veteran's race in Europe, with the advantage that this was always an agreeable place to visit. The last stage of this race which was held in September always finished in Grevenmacher, thus usually having the advantage of coinciding with the wine festival. Not unsurprisingly, I gleaned a little knowledge of the Luxemburg wines which were predominantly the white varieties. I can however recommend a red-the Pinot noir, which usually is excellent. Wines were usually priced and listed in order of the cheapest varieties first, by the wine traders at this festival, the order was roughly as follows:

1/ *EBLING* the oldest variety 2/ *PINOT GRE and PINOT BLANC* 3/ *CHARDONAY* 4/ *RIESLING and SYLVANER* 5/ *GEWURZTRAMINER and MUSCAT* the sweat wines.

At this time, there was still sort of a customs border, which was to give us great amusement the day we stayed in a hotel at the German side of the bridge in Grevenmacher.

Unfortunately, not to Dave at the time, perhaps now in retrospect. I suppose we stayed in this hotel because it was cheaper, it turned out to be very un-German like, they were very disorganised. In the evening after the race, our team strolled over the bridge back into Luxembourg, I stress this was before the wine festival. As the common market was not fully functional, there was still a sentry in his box at the end of the bridge; we assumed he was there to check on goods. All the time we had been there, we never saw the sentry even move a muscle. That is till Dave strolling behind attempted to cross along with all the locals. We know Dave can be looked on suspiciously, as we all can, watching and waiting for him to catch us up on the Luxembourg side. To our surprise, he was challenged by the sentry to produce his passport, all our passports were back in the hotel. There was quite a confrontation, Dave was jumping up and down, the sentry unslinging his rifle. All he had to do was go back and cross on the footbridge 50 yards away, where there was no sentry or go back and obtain his passport, the confrontation was better than going to the pantomime. ***Did we vote for Brexit? I don't think so!***

Another time when travelling to this race by car with a full team, the last rider to be picked up was Sandy Cairns. This rider we knew from his attacking rides in the Peter Friar races, where he had a tendency to disappear early down the road on a suicide mission. It was arranged that we picked him up outside another rider's house, who was away at the time in Gravesend, where he was leaving his car while we were away. On arrival, he was dozing in his car, leaving him to fix his bike on the car roof we set off, but no, the bike was not fixed; it almost fell off, thinking he was still half asleep, we fixed it.

On the journey to Dover, he was still unresponsive; on arrival, he was incapable of waking up properly to find his passport, we did musical passports to pass the customs, leaving him alone on the ferryboat. During the journey, not much changed in his comportment till our arrival at the hotel. This was half way to Luxembourg, where I collected the rather large keys for everyone's rooms. The first time I realised there was something drastically wrong was when he tried to open the car door with the room key; two minutes later, he had collapsed on the floor in a fit. At the hospital, I had a hell of a job in explaining the situation to the staff as you would imagine, all we knew of Sandy was that he was a research chemist and lived alone. From his wallet, we found a phone number, his racing licence some money, but no passport. On telephoning his lodger, he could shed no light on the situation, but thought he had a problem, collapsing a couple of weeks earlier.

The hospital staff were brilliant, notwithstanding their perplexity in not knowing much about our team mate. It transpired after all the tests that he had not been taking his medication for a condition that we had no suspicion of. Our conclusion rightly or wrongly, was that he had saved up the medication with disastrous results; this time, to have a bigger dose when he was racing, which maybe explained to us his style of riding. Fortunately, the hospital normalised him as much as possible during his brief séjour. Following his wishes, we took him to the nearest railway station to make his way home, leaving his bike to collect later, which he did this time with a passport. It was then rather a rush to make it in time for the first stage of the race, where somehow, I achieved my best result on this first stage after competing in this race seven times. Perhaps, it was telling me something? I wish I knew what.

During the very last time I rode this tour, it rained every day. The number of horrendous crashes in this race made the current Tour de France, with all the roadwork furniture crashes look benign by comparison; many of the crashes were because of the reckless speeds descending and into bends despite the atrocious conditions. This turned out to be the last race in this form. My belief is that the organisers thought the same as me, that the reckless riding was as a result of wanting to obtain result at all costs, or riders been rather befuddled in their heads because of what they had taken, I can only surmise. I have no proof.

Tour De Mallorca

I rode and finished in seven Tours of Mallorca the same number of times I had ridden in the Tour of Luxembourg. I along with all the riders in the team had more success in the Tour de Mallorca admirably assisted by Bill Cheadle as mechanic throughout. He became just at home in Mallorca as he was in Rotherham. The first time we had a team in this race, our impression was that we were tolerated by the organisation, not exactly encouraged. They had not yet embraced foreigners; only in so far as to assist them in their own teams. The local team from the Establements Club certainly meant business, they had engaged a proven 35-year-old Frenchman into their team, with this leader they went on to dominate the race. Of course, this was a senior rider's race for over 40s; they made a rule that local riders under this age could ride, the Frenchman was not local, but no matter. It certainly was a tough race taking in the climbs at Galilea, Capdelia, Puigpunyent, Esporles, Valdemosso all in the western part of the island where the scenery was absolutely stunning, although we did not have the opportunity to gaze around. Our team rode very well, we were not disgraced, despite being at the wrong end of the age scale. Finally, the prize presentation was held on the last night in a rather sumptuous local palace. This was the only time this location was used. Perhaps, it was because on this occasion some of the proceedings were filmed for the TV. Pete Mathews, one of our star riders, as many know he purports to be an entertainer or comedian, he wrapped himself up in toilet paper like an Egyptian mummy, not a dead one, as he was rolling round the floor completely ignored by everyone. We had to drag him away; he completely misunderstood the situation, it was not as if they did not have a sense of humour, rather they wanted the limelight to be completely Mallorcan. Even a 30-year-old local who finished last in the race received a trophy as tall as he was. To alleviate our hurt feelings, several members of the Basque team who had seen our team's heroic efforts, went to the presentation table, forcibly collecting several trophies presenting them to us.

Pedro Canals, the owner of the Sant Diego and Solimar Hotels in Arenal, provided our team with the food and accommodation for the week, as he always did for all the tours we rode in. We stayed in the budget hotel receiving the food of the first-class hotel. Sometimes, there were other guests in our hotel. On one occasion, I had to stay an extra day because of flight timings. Next day, when the food reverted to the normal level, the look on the faces of the two or three guests remaining was something else. I would describe it as the look of sad mice. After this first tour, we were treated very differently; it was as if they had suddenly woken up to the fact that the island prospered because of tourism, or Pedro had kicked them up the butt. Normally, the race organisation was pretty good, especially the police traffic control. The organisers did have their slip ups, the crème de la crème of slip ups occurred when the stage start was in Santa Maria, on completing perhaps 40 km into the stage at the sea front at Cala Millor we were stopped. Jack Wright and myself were in a small lead group. Small groups of riders continued to arrive behind us; it was just like waves crashing onto the shore, just as relentless. They gave the explanation that the officials had become lost and needed to catch up with the race. The simple truth was they had lingered too long in the bar after the race start, drinking their coffee and brandy. When the race restarted, it again split into similar groups as previously; you can take it that the relentless pace of the first 40 km was ongoing, a similar distance was added to the total for the stage, resulting in Jack and myself finishing at the front of the race in the fading light.

Dave Marsh was not so lucky, or perhaps he was, appearing in the dark sometime later with a police motor cyclist on either side with full headlights and horns blaring. Somehow, not surprisingly, Jack Wright being small with a low-profile style was missed from the result. They promised to rectify this, despite our entreaties for the rest of the race, regrettably, no rectification was made.

On one occasion, the stage finish was outside the local liquor brewery. Afterwards, we were invited inside to the showroom, where we were offered the local liquor at a special price; the problem was the same stuff was available in the local stores at a lower price.

Another stage which finished in Binaili was not so dry; immediately after crossing the finishing line, a torrential downpour only drenched the bunch amazingly for the last 200 meters. I was just in front of the bunch riding through the open door of the local bar just after the finishing line, not getting wet or disqualified, but gaining a quick drink as well as a few seconds, to the great amusement of the locals in the bar.

Descending the Solar Pass on another stage from the Palma side, I was a victim of the oil from the crushed olives on the bend, that had fallen off the tree. The same olives you put with the liquor. Having a long chase on the climb on the coast road towards Andraix, before I regained my group. This was the only crash I had in the seven times of riding this tour. Ken Cowdell after helping me to remain with the leaders on the Col d' Honor, the climb from Alaro to Bunyola, fell off on the last bend into Orient village, losing his chance of winning the stage. Ken did have his stage win on the day the race finished in Son Ferriol. He was away for the last 30 km with a German, beating him in the sprint. It was at this finish that we were to witness another crash on this very hot sunny day. Most of our team, including our mechanic Bill Cheadle, sat enjoying an ice cream, when we saw Barry Clarke come rolling head over heels across the finishing line in a big cloud of dust sprinting for 90th place. Well, what can you say?

Crashes were not the only hazard; mosquitoes were another one. In the night at our hotel, two teammates Gaz Hill and Steve Gresley were almost eaten alive. Steve was the worst affected, Gaz had no spare fat, so the mosquitoes did not have much to bite on; instead they turned their attention on the unfortunate Steve, where his racing shorts finished on his legs, it looked as if someone had gone round his leg with a knitting machine. Not so, it was the mosquito bites, not having any hair on his head, he was so badly bitten there; he had to go to the hospital for treatment. Being a tough Yorkshireman, he was on the starting line the next day. Gaz was to suffer another indignity another year, despite being resplendent in his national veterans championship jersey. He was the current road race champion this particular year, when he was asked to relinquish his front place on the starting line. This was for a rider who was better known for being first on another kind of starting grid. It was to make way for Alain Prost, four times World Formula 1 Motor Racing champion. I bet you did not know he raced on a bike; he was not bad either. At 43 years of age, it was to be expected, as we are told you have to be very fit for Formula 1 motor racing.

In total, I had two stage wins, one in the atmospheric setting of the Place D' Espagne in the Centre of Palma, where I won the criterium on a Sunday, being the only day possible to hold this race in the city. A close rival often in these races was Jack Watson. At the start of a time trial stage at Lloret, we were both well placed in the general classification. Jack had his supporters, some of whom came asking me if I was worried about the time trial, no doubt thinking their man might have the advantage. They soon changed their mind when I told them I had ridden a 10 at home the last weekend doing a short 21 on my road bike, which was a few seconds outside an age record, which I know it is slow by today's standards. Winning this time trial was to be a big help in my finishing third on general classification for the second time. The overall winner was the Dutch rider JJ Van Kessel; it also was his second win; later he received a doping ban. When his ban was completed, and he was back again riding the Tour De Mallorca, it was noticeable that now he was not climbing as well. Big Dutchmen are generally not noted to be good climbers; there are exceptions.

In the last two tours I competed, there were too many riders, resulting in the organisers in their wisdom, deciding to have an over the age of 50 section. This was not a bad idea; the execution of it was, by setting off the over 50 riders in a separate bunch and integrating them with main body of the race after 30 kilometres had been completed. This was a badly thought out and a dangerous exercise; I refused to take part in this. Riding the main over the age of 40 race, from the start, I still managed to finish fourth overall on general classification. Stupidly, they decided the same format again the following year, refusing me permission to ride the full distance. This was to be my last time; I never wanted to take part in it again.

Buying Property in France 1990

In 1990, when my business had been established 20 years, Janet and myself bought our first property in Brittany. This was at St-Quay-Portrieux, not too far from St Brieuc on the coast in the Cotes De Goello. For part of the year, this was our residence, as I was able to direct much of my business from this base. Now with the Covid pandemic, working from home is becoming more prevalent. Not only in the UK are more people working this way; here in Brittany too, this is happening. As I write this at the end of September 2020, living in Plouha, Cotes de D'Amor, it is very difficult to buy or rent a property. Only nine months ago, there were a lot of properties for sale with few buyers. Suddenly, people from the big cities wanted to live in the countryside. This area of Brittany has quickly become in huge demand. For an area with a population of 4,000 people, we all at once have seven estate agents, most of whom will be out of business in two years' time. In the year 2000, we had a new house built, in an adjacent village, then spending even more time in France.

By the year 2005, we had permanently moved to France, paying our taxes in this country. During all this time, I still had a racing license with the Velo Club de Quintin, racing in the local events. These races were all on circuits with an average distance of 100 km; a few were longer. The finishing line was almost always in the centre of the local village or town, the number of laps ranged from eight to twenty. Some races were shorter, around 80 km; they had even more laps and were super-fast. To ride place to place races or stage races, you had to be a first category rider, or a younger rider in a team. In these types of races, the organisers were looking to give the younger riders not holding a first category license more experience. In the criteriums. I did not try to win primes, more important was the training for bigger international races, so the main thing was to complete the distance. At best I could very occasionally finish fourth or fifth; more realistically, I aimed to be in the first 10. I sort of became a regular fixture in these races, where I saw the likes of Sebastian Hinault and Cyril Gaughter come through the junior ranks. Both of them becoming stalwarts of the Tour de France.

I rode a few races in the Normandy area, mostly in the Louvigne du Desert, St Hilaire du Harcoue region. These races tended to be longer distances, with long drags (faux plat' in French) as opposed to the steeper climbs in the Cotes D'Amor.

One of the super-fast criteriums was the one held in Saint Malo, near the train station. This event started at 5 pm on a weekday in the middle of the summer when the tourists were about, consequently drawing good crowds. This race was open to second, third and fourth categories, plus the junior categories, consisting of 40 very tricky laps. You had to be very watchful of the juniors in this type of super-fast race, as they did not have the experience with the speed. It was a race you did better in if you had previously competed on this circuit. Most unusually, there was a prize for the first placed veteran. My biggest competitor for this prize was Andre Foucher (eight Tour de France's completed, twice winning the Mid-Libre); he was five years older than me. He won the first time I rode, then I beat him the following year.

Tour of Bavaria
(Bayern Rundfahrt) June 1987

In June 1987, as a mere 49-year-old, I organised a team to ride a 6-day 7-stages race in Bavaria in the masters category. This was the International Bayern Rundfahrt attracting national teams from Holland, Switzerland, Italy, Denmark, Austria, even a mixed team from Czechoslovakia and Austria, plus several regional and club teams. Our team comprised of Jack Wright, Denis Hill, Dave Marsh and myself. Dale Coen was the very capable assistant who was essential to the team. We flew to Austria where I hired a car. The race started at Lenggries high on the Austrian border, the same town that is twined with my neighbouring village of Plelo on the Cotes de Goello. As is the case with many of these twinings, I have never heard of much being organised. Perhaps, this is just as well as my village Plouha is twinned with Seix in the Pyrenees; I have never heard of any activities that I can talk about with this twinning. Twining and Seix is enough of a subject without going any further.

As the start, was at a high altitude; you would expect the race to be all downhill. Probably it was, but not for the total of 124 km of the stage. In fact, it was extremely fast, too fast in fact for our youngest rider of a mere 35-year-old, Dave

Marsh. Dave was very confident of his chances considering his age advantage, youth proved to be no substitute for experience. Unfortunately, he was eliminated, not being helped by his breakfast, which had not agreed with him, finishing outside the time limit.

Second day, we had a team time trial starting at the civilised time of 10.00 am. Over the short distance of 19.4 km, arriving at the finish the best news for us was that we were not last. Even better news was my wallet was returned which I had left behind on the starting ramp. Yes, it was a big race we had a starting ramp.

Third stage was a 25 lap, 50 km criterium in the picturesque medieval town of Auerback. A 6.00 pm start attracting the Sunday afternoon sightseers. This proved to be an intelligent arrangement as the crowds were huge. They were well entertained, the race being very fast on a tricky partly cobbled circuit circumventing a Benedictine monastery in the confines of the town centre. We had to use all our skill and experience to even survive in the bunch. Towards the end of the race, we confided in one another, that we were feeling more confident, thinking we had a good chance in the finish. True to our sensations, we were well placed crossing the line for the finishing sprint. It was only after going to see the result that we learned it had been a points race. This explained everything, a pity no one informed us of this in English. It would have made no difference to the result if we had known.

Problems started with Denis at the finish, he was usually our best finisher in the Tour of Luxemburg. His problem was not in the legs but in the head. First, he thought it normal to prance around in the street after he had stripped naked to change. This was a very busy street with the crowds heading home for their schnaps. The crowds being Bavarian appeared to be not too bothered, but we were. Perhaps, they thought it all part of the street entertainment. Our hotel and breakfasts were paid for by the organizers, we paid for the rest of the meals. Denis refused to discuss the financial problems he was obviously having, neither did he want to talk about any assistance we could give him. Regrettably, he decided to do his own thing, eating alone and apart. Next morning, when we arrived for breakfast, Denis had been and gone. Our breakfast that had been laid out for us looked rather sparse.

Fourth Stage Waldershof-90 km. Although a short stage, this was another hard day of racing, with good crowds and helicopters overhead following the race. I doubt if they recorded much of us. Dave not taking part in the race, set off to ride the route alone for much needed training. No Dave at the finish since he was lost. Even worse, he was many miles off route with no idea of how to reach Waldershof. Luckily, he had the luck of the Irish even though he was not Irish, probably Scotch. He found someone, perhaps the only person in Bavaria admitting to being able to speak English, bringing him and his bike to the finish. On arriving at the hotel, Denis preceded us, carrying a wooden tray in front of him like a tray full of vegetables you would buy at the market. Not the comportment for a guest arriving at a four-star hotel. Despite this, keeping a straight face, as four star-doormen are trained to do, he opened the door as if Denis was Angel Merkle. Denis again dined alone as we finally realised the tray's contents were part of our breakfast.

Fifth Stage Strullendort-110 km.

This was a very wet day with some nasty crosswinds. I was off the pace of the leaders in a group of about 20 riders.

Some very smart rider, he must have been a local turned us left at a forked junction. It as I suspected turned out to be not the route of the race, but we regained the bunch again. At the finish, we received a 5 min. penalty, which was very generous as in reality, we would have lost even more time. That night, the hotel failed to find us anywhere to leave our bikes. They remained strapped on top of the car in the rain; the management having assured us they were safe. Next day, I mentioned this to Peter Baur in the Czech/Austrian team, who I had often competed against. We had a good relationship he was born in Czechoslovakia, but lived and worked in Austria. His reply was that's nothing, it happened to us at a remote mountain location in the Tour of Corsica. When we told the hosts, we were worried about bandits stealing our bikes, the reply was, "Don't worry, we are the bandits round here." It was Peter who had his photo taken on the Podium when I won, the criterium stage in the centre of Palma in the Tour De Mallorca. He had to give me the trophy back when the result was reversed after consulting the photo finish.

Sixth Stage Rothenburg-95 km.

We all negotiated the finish through the clocktower arch; the narrow entrance into the town. What a wonderful setting for a stage race finish into Germany's best-preserved medieval town. This town was especially known for its architecture and half-timbered houses. On this stage, we had an early start finishing at about 2.00 pm. What a delightful place to be for the rest of the day.

Seventh Stage Weibenburg-103 km.

This was a day of high winds often gusting very strongly which split the peloton to smithereens. Echelon after echelon formed using the full width of the tarmac as the roads were closed to traffic. I was in a rear echelon where Theo Kanal, who was back in circulation, sat at the front, doing all the work. When I asked a big Dutchman (I had a habit of sitting on big Dutchmen's wheels in the wind), "if we should give him some help."

"No," he replied in perfect English, "he is that doped up, it will not make any difference; leave him be." It was well known that Theo had been previously suspended after failing a doping test. Arriving at the finishing town through a very impressive drawbridge one could imagine the drawbridge, being raised a la Belge, if you were outside the time limit. Often in Belgium, if you were 10 minutes behind the leaders no matter how big the group was, you were pulled out of the race. No, we made it to the finish, once recovered, we could appreciate this old city which had once been a free Imperial City for 500 years. The town history dates back to an old Roman fort built in the first century. One of the icons of the city is the Old Town Hall, often referred to as the Rasthausen. Often in many towns in Europe, it is the Rasthausen where you sign on at the start of a race, this is referred to by the riders as the rat house, as this is the nearest, we came to the correct pronunciation.

After the prize presentation where we did not have a lot to shout about, it was back to the hotel where we were more than ready for the evening meal. The dining room was styled as Bavarian eating halls have been fashioned for perhaps hundreds of years. Everywhere, there were crossed swords, shields, stuffed animal heads, very long tables, high backed chairs, with decorations and paraphernalia to match. Being our last night, we were able to drink more; in addition, we were ready for a change of menu to the taga soup and apple strudel we had been eating most days. It was only later that we learned taga soup was the soup of the day and apple strudel was the only desert we could understand on the menu. Unfortunately, the service was rather slow. It appeared that the people in the basement where loud music, singing, shouting and laughter were coming from, were receiving the service, not us. On investigating, this dining room was even more elaborate than ours. There was a very long table at which were seated a group of older men. They were all well inebriated, shouting and banging their beer steins on the table. To all appearances, they were a revival meeting of the Third Reich. It was abundantly clear that we did not command the same authority, determined to rectify this, I returned to my room donning my golf club blazer. This was rather an official looking garment like the green jacket, presented to the winner of the Masters Golf Tournament. Mine had an elaborate captain's badge on the pocket, attired thus I went back to the bar giving it a good thumping; this did the trick; the service was immaculate after that. It was what the French would call "Prestige de Costume," I have no idea why I took this blazer with me. Later, I was to learn that following the second World War, 6,000 people expelled from Germany's former territories were re-settled in this city, no doubt, the most important among them were in the bar that night.

Travelling back to the airport, we were mean enough to refuse Denis the Menace a lift. Halfway on route, a convoy of brand-new BMW cabrioles, that had been used as official vehicles in the race swept by us at a great speed. In the last one was Denis with two of the hostess girls and his bike draped on the back. Maybe we did it wrong; we should have cavorted naked at the finish. The following year, I received an invitation to send a team again, which I declined; perhaps, it was Denis that was the attraction not our team. Two years later, the race was upgraded to a professional race, I think we were the guinea pigs to fine tune the organisation.

Having some time on hand before my flight left Munich Airport, I had time to ride my bike round the city centre. What was very impressive, apart from the city itself was the ease of use of the bike lanes which were everywhere. Not far from the centre, I even found my way to an area set aside for allotments. These were as good if not better than any I have ever seen elsewhere, a little Tranquille paradise.

France Cyclo Sportives Discovered

When I was in my late 40s, early 50s, I was introduced to cyclo-sportives which had started to grow in popularity. There were of course the Randonnée's which were not competitive and the sportives which were. For many, they were extremely important, some of the pros rode them. For others like me, they were a welcome addition to the criterium races. There were cyclists who had never raced who discovered they had the talent for these sportives, some a few, were as good as the best couriers. Fortunately, I have never crashed in a sportive. However, you had to be very wary of your fellow competitor's bike handling skills and experience, luck also plays its part. Although the roads are closed for the leaders, you cannot rely on they will remain closed, especially further into the event. If you are off the pace, it is more than likely they will be closed. When there are accidents, which inevitably there are, the ambulances must follow the direction of the race traffic before they reach the scene.

In these competitions, stamina was not a problem, as I was doing the mileage needed at that time. For me, the advantage was that the starts were slower, especially with the longer events. With the passing of the years, you have a need to ride yourself in. With the shorter sportives, the competitors were not afraid of the distance; so they started quicker. Over the years, the distances have been reduced, which has had the effect of making the starts quicker than they used to be, or perhaps it is my imagination, but I don't think so. In truth, the same principal applies in normal racing. However, in one cyclo-sportive at Laval the speed was regulated for the first one and a half hours, the total distance being 190 km. This was the Philip Dalibard in 1988 in honour of the well-known pro and current team manager; the event not the speed restriction. At one point in the event, we had to walk over the top of a hill, just as I had once done over Fleet Moss. The organisers found this narrow steep brute of a climb where only the first five or six riders made it over the top, helped by the bottleneck behind. Just the sort of thing Bernard Hinault tried to do in his sportives. I suppose the organisers wanted to show that the terrain in this area of the Alps Mancelles was not for pussy cats. The result of this was that it was a long hard chase to reel in the leaders again. For my pains, I was to finish sixth in a time of 5.54.20 an average speed of 32 kmph which was not bad with the slow start.

On my birthday-5 July 1998, I managed to win the Jean Marie Goasmat sportive. This was a shortish distance of 136 km in the Pays de Pluvigner, Morbihan, beating all the younger riders; this was not a birthday present. The young guy who was second was rather peeved, to put it mildly. He complained not only to the announcer (speaker) but to all and sundry about being robbed. The complaint was I had sat on his wheel for the long drag up to the finish and had the cheek to come by him on the finishing line. His stalwart effort up the long finishing drag had reduced those remaining to a very long single line. The announcer was Jean Gillet, who had often carried out the same function, when I was competing in earlier days. This complaint made the day for Jean Gillet telling him, "Didn't you know it was Neale Gordon sat on your wheel; this should be a lesson to you not to take chances with riders of his experience."

Footnote: Jean-Marie Goasmat a Breton, had competed in eight Tour de France; amazingly he had raced continually from 1934 to 1954 even throughout WW2.

It was myself who made a bad error in another sportive, when I failed to make allowances for female sensitivities. The error was not at the sportive but a week later, when I was introduced to Geraldine Gill who was the multiple lady's road racing champion of Ireland. This was at a social occasion at my club. She was asked if she had met or knew Neale Gordon? "No," she said. Stupidly, I said, "You finished just behind me in the Guy Ignolin sportive last Saturday." She looked at this old guy, me, saying, "No, impossible," very indignantly. The facts were that she was just on my wheel at the finish; I won my age category in a time of 3.43.20, Geraldine won the ladies category in a time of 3.43.21. My current clubmate Michel Aubrey Aubree winning in a younger category, 15 seconds quicker than myself. No, I should have simply replied we were in the same sportive last week, that would have been sufficient. This sportive was held in 1998 over 140 km in the Cotes de Granit Rose, this beautiful area of Brittany. The coastal rocks are a pink colour, hence the name. It is understandable Geraldine was rather peeved with my remark, she was commended in the press for finishing with the elite riders, 5 minutes behind the winner, Jean-Phillippe Rouxel in a time of 3.38.00.

In truth, I have raced with some good ladies, when they were allowed to ride in the UK local events, Lisa Brambini, Katty Allen, who not only had the results, but could handle a bike better than most of the men. On my training camp in Mallorca, on one occasion, I was the only older rider remaining on the climb towards Deia from Solar, all the other older riders had been blown out by a talented group of ladies. This group included Maxine Johnson, Vicky Thomas, Katty, Zoey among others.

The big cyclo-sportive in Brittany is the Pierre La Bigault, based at Callac, organised in aid of the Mucoviscidosis relief fund. Regularly about 10,000 participants take part in this; the main event is a sportive with a results classification and two shorter distance Randonnée's. This is another event where Aubrey Aubree won winning in the younger category to mine, 15 seconds quicker than myself. No, I should have simply re they have now cut the distances down. When I rode my first one, the distance was just over 200 km. I was disappointed in finishing 44th. In the terrain around Callac, this is never easy. From year to year, the route varies; some routes are harder than others, they are all tough in this part of the world. On the second time of my participation, I slipped to 48th, so I decided I would ride the shorter distances in the future, which were a mere 110-120 km.

Another real tester was the Costamorican of 1995, Dinan to Lannion (Re-named L'etape de Tour). This was a duplicate of the 235 km Tour de France stage, held the Saturday before, having been won by the Italian Baldato in front of Jalabert and Adoujaparov. As I have said before, Brittany is not flat, this stage hugged the coast for much of the route, in essence dropping into river and the watercourse valleys, before climbing out again, one after another. There were also the long hard drags, such as the one where you really found it hard to cope with the wind at cap Frehel. Also, on the route was the steep brute of a climb from the port of Brehec, the Breton Mur de Grammont, without the cobbles. My friend Jack Wright came over to ride with me, at 30 km to go, we were both well enough placed together to have a result. Unfortunately, I punctured at this point, losing a lot of time trying to change a tubular. Jack had the pleasure in winning his age category. This event proved to be so popular it was re-run the following year, where I won my category, but it was not the same as winning the original.

Peter Fryer Trophy Series

I rode in many of the Peter Fryer Trophy National Series, the over 40 series in the beginning, later, in the over 50 series. It was obviously an advantage if you were nearer the eligibility age, a 50-year-old would be giving an advantage of 10 years to a 40-year-old, this is a lot in cycling. Always the first race in the series was on the Eastway Circuit in East London. After initially giving it a try, I soon decided, it was held too early in the season; subsequently, giving this race a miss. The next one was usually in the Halifax area, where it was also quite cold over the Yorkshire moors early season. On several occasions, I could not cope with the cold, when returning to the headquarters after abandoning, it was not uncommon for other abandoned riders to complain that something had gone wrong with their bike. The headset was vibrating; going downhill was the usual excuse, of course, there was nothing wrong with the bike, it was the cold. All too often, car boot sales were organised on some of the circuits we used, too much traffic becoming a problem, another circuit had to be found, usually an answer was found, but not always.

In one race, three of us travelled together from the north for a race near Gravesend. As the three of us, Jack Wright, who was my usual companion and Collin Davidson, better known as a mountain biker, had eaten the same meal in an Indian restaurant the evening before. We finished one two three in this over 40 Peter Fryer. I do not know if this meal, or the fact that I may have taken the wrong bidon, had any bearing on this surprising result.

Always there was a good banter with many of the colourful characters that participated in these races. One of these was John Marshall; he owned a furniture business called Durham Pine. Being a Geordie, he did not waste money on actors to do his television commercials, acting the part himself. His arrivals at the competitions were also exotic, with a dolly bird on his arm, driving a rare Rolls Royce, a specially converted 4-door Silver Shadow. It is easy to understand why he had the nickname Hulio Geordio, after the Spanish singer Julio Iglesias. One day, he arrived for the race with a face like a sad mouse. When asked what was wrong, he replied, "Her at home wants a divorce," to which, quick as a flash Jack replied, "**Oh! you will only be half a millionaire now.**" He was not the only one with a vintage car, others preferred to be more discreet, with the car, I don't know about girlfriends. Jack himself had two working Lagonda's plus three other Lagonda Chaises that he was working on, one quite rare. Ken Cowdell owned a Bentley S3 Continental Mulliner Flying Spur; he kept this to take his wife Margaret to rallies, including the prestigious Monte Carlo Rally.

One year, I had the trophy for the most points for a rider over 50 in the over 40 series. Another year, in 1990 in the actual over 50 races, I was fourth with 300 points to the winner's Brian Rourke's 337 points; he had ridden all eight of the qualifying races, of which your best five results were to count, I had ridden in only five of the races.

It paid to be prudent by not trying to race if you were unwell. This I was to prove, after doing a certified randonais, the full length of the Pyrenees, from the north to the south, finishing at Cerbere. This included many of the tougher Tour de France Mountain climbs. It was quite tough completing the distance in the allocated time, not to Peter Wilsons Highgate club members who I was accompanying. Although there were times when it became very tough for some of the group. I recall at one point, some athletes on roller skates passed some of us going uphill. They did not have the luxury of being able to benefit like we could, on the downhills, they all mounted in the minibus which was accompanying them. On one morning, I was not feeling so good, having some sort of cold; I put my bike in the vehicle that was accompanying us. My companions were rather taken aback at this, pointing out that I would not receive the certificate for completing the ride. Not that I was bothered about the certificate, more about my form, I am pretty sure I would not have won the Peter Fryer at St Albans the following weekend if I had ridden that morning when I was unwell.

At one Peter Fryer in 1988, the dreadful news was received on our arrival at the start, that Ron Coe had died in the night of a heart attack. He was 55, having been training for his first comeback race since he retired as a professional in the Viking Truman Steel team. What a shock to those calling to bring him to his veterans' inauguration race, as it was to the rest of us, especially me as we had shared much together. Ron had been four times national road race champion; three of them as BLRC national champion, sadly, Bronco's galloping days were over.

Mountain Biking

To make a change to normal club runs, the Doncaster section of the Dinnington Club organised ourselves riding mountain bikes in the winter. This proved to be the initiation for me taking up mountain bike competitions, which was a new challenge. I found I could win competitions on the faster circuits in Clumber Park and Sherwood Forest, which was quite rewarding and a new experience. Being a person not shy in trying to progress, a natural evolution was in competing in the Mountain Biking National Series. I competed in these races for three years. Mick Ives gave me some tips on how to negotiate the terrain in these events. With his experience, no one was better qualified. How to select a line through the corners whilst keeping the distance shorter and not going outside the boundaries of the circuit helped. From time to time, I could finish in the top six on the faster circuit. On the rocky technical courses, I was not as good. Starting these races at an older age you are acutely aware that if you crash on the rocky terrain, it will do much damage. It never entered my head that I could just as easily wrap myself around a tree. I must have had confidence in my bike handling.

A well-known Midlands circuit proved trickier than most circuits. It was a wet muddy day for this 3-lap race. The first lap, I gingerly descended through the quarry, then I picked up some further places on the climb up to the folly monument. Then, the second lap through the quarry, I had the fright of my life descending like a lunatic through the quarry. This is what you have to do in these events, but I was not ready to kick my clogs just yet. When I arrived at the finishing line with still one lap to go, I discovered my brake blocks were completely worn away. To be told that you need special brake blocks here as there is an abrasive in the quarry mud that wears normal ones away. Thanks, I replied; I can do without a fright like that I am certainly not doing the last lap without brakes. Nowadays, the disc brakes that have been in use for a long time now solve that problem. When the master categories were introduced, I certainly could not compete with 30-year-olds. That being the end of that adventure. I must also confess I did not like being held in a compound for half an hour before the race started, especially if it was pouring with rain.

I did continue to ride my mountain bike in Brittany purely for pleasure. At this time, mountain biking or VTT velo tout terrain giving it its French name was just taking off. It has since become hugely popular in France. Where I now live in Brittany, we have the highest cliffs in the region. The tracks that run the length of the coast, as well as inland are absolutely magnificent. Especially the breath-taking views from the cliff tops. In addition, if you wish to give these tracks a try when you are on holiday, the routes are well indicated. Most of the tourist offices have special maps available free of charge.

Russian World Road Race Championship for Veterans

The plan was that three of us would travel to Russia to participate in the Eastern Blocks version of the Veterans World Road Race Championships. Unfortunately, Jack Wright's visa failed to arrive in time; so, there was just Bob Theis and myself. He was Arthur Metcalf's look alike, on Bob's own admission when it came to racing, he was just a pale shadow of the real Arthur. Never having ridden against Arthur, another great Yorkshireman, I was aware of his record, including winning the British road race championship and best all-rounder in the same year. As Bob did not come from Yorkshire but nonetheless a respected rider from Bristol, I had no doubt about his admission.

At the airport seeing a group of barefooted monks in white robes boarding the aircraft for the second leg of our flight to Moscow, I started to wonder what we were letting ourselves in for. After all, Russia is a communist country. On arrival, we were met by the race organiser who said he was not going with us to Muron (Mypom), where the racing was to be held, 600 km. to the east. He still had some business to attend to in Moscow, claiming Muron was chosen as the venue as it was out of the control of the Mafia.

It was arranged; we stayed in Moscow, taking the train the next day. As a bonus, we received the grand sight-seeing tour, the Kremlin, Red Square all was exactly as you see on films and TV. Then we visited a superstore, the Harrods of Moscow without the class; their admission was limited to people with special passes. Every luxury we were able to buy in the west was available here and more besides, only for purchases in dollars. This was not a place for the masses or us; we could not afford to buy anything. Continuing on our visit, we travelled on the underground, seeing what are undoubtedly the most beautiful metro stations in the world. Among several which were noteworthy, we saw one which resembled a cathedral below ground, they were all clean and tidy. It was the opposite when we exited the metro. Climbing the long stairs to the daylight, many women and young boys were trying to sell puppies and dogs. At least I thought they don't eat them in Russia; I later had my doubts with the food we were given.

Then we had the parade down the main shopping street with all the restaurants or what was left of them. Every alternate one was a blackened ruin; some of them still smouldering, the work of the Mafia I was told. These sights were an endorsement of why we were going to be hot tailing it east. No hotel for us the first night; it seemed to us that the race organiser was trying to make enough money to flee to the west. This was what many of the people we were subsequently to meet wanted to do. Accommodation was arranged for us in one of the massive white painted apartment blocks, again exactly as you see on the TV. We were well looked after and comfortable enough. I imagine they were similar inside to the massive flats you see on the hill dwarfing the centre of Sheffield, even though I have never set foot in one. Next morning, we were not to hot foot it east but rather slow coach it, as we were told all the trains were full, probably a ruse to make more money.

Muron and the surrounding areas were a centre for armaments manufacture and a strategic railway centre. The railways were of vital importance in the Second World War, although throughout our sojourn, I cannot recall ever having seen any railways. Perhaps, explained by the concentration needed in racing when you are practically oblivious of the scenery. There were two drivers on the coach; all we saw for hour after hour was endless pine forest. On arriving in the town, we passed a long row of metal cabins with just a door. These belonged to the shopkeepers who were selling fruit and vegetables, scabby looking apples, manky looking potatoes plus other inedible looking products. At the bus depot, we asked where the main street was, to be told that was the main street. In Moscow, all the vehicles seemed to be brand new or very old, there did not seem to be anything in between. Here, in Muron, mostly the vehicles to be seen were rusty looking lorries of various sizes, tankers, etc., still in camouflage colours, seemingly of WW2 vintage.

Ok; onwards to the hotel; the only hotel in the area was directly in front of the chemical works. During the whole time we were lodged here, we were never free from the aroma of diesel and other chemicals. For the everyday visitors to this hotel, it was very practical as they were here to visit these works. At last, we were free to explore on our bikes; it's called training, Leaving the very neglected looking apartments in the town, arriving on the outskirts, people were living in dilapidated single storey rough-hewn log cabins, many with broken windows. They all had large shutters, presumably to keep the cold out during the winters, which we were told were not very pleasant. Finally, we discovered there was a nice scenic area down by the river. Keen to explore further, we did not see any buildings of any description, only a large boat moored to the bank. We climbed on the boat, on entering the large metal cabin and going inside this was open to the river. Later, we were told this served as a swimming pool for the youngsters. The next night we were taken to a sports complex that was fairly modern, especially after everything else we had seen. Here, we were to witness the cycling week's opening ceremony which was quite impressive for a town of this size, situated in the backwoods. The local children were dressed in the local area's traditional costumes; they marched round the track of the arena playing instruments and juggling etc. All this was very well rehearsed and presented, others paraded models and depictions of their local heroes and villains. Horses, swords, battledresses, shields, dragons etc. were all involved; we did not understand completely but got the gist of things. I suppose they were their equivalents of our Robin Hood and Richard the Lionheart.

After that we visited the local crafts market, standards varied, but we were impressed with much that we saw, Russian dolls, embroidery, ceramics; unusually, there were many items that initially you thought were ceramics, on closer inspection they were fashioned or carved in wood and hand painted; these items seemed to be a speciality of this market. Some bargains were to be had, everything was modestly priced provided you paid in dollars, they would also accept the German mark, the British Pound was a no no; I think they were trying to tell us something. We bought a few things that could be carried. We were always being stopped and given little trinkets; even worse, we were forever offered drinks of vodka from a flask produced from the depth of their clothing. The men insisted that we had to taste their own special vodka, we had to pretend to have a slip in order not to offend them; this was more difficult because some had consumed an adequate amount of this tiple already. Their reaction to a refusal would have been rather unpredictable. It is likely that if we had drunk their vodka, it would not have done us any good, but not intentionally. All this was explained by the fact the area had been closed to westerners up to the year before, it being an important armaments area, they had their first visitors only the previous year. In the village where the road race started, they had never seen any westerners, the first to come into contact with them were a bunch of cyclists. Perhaps, they thought all westerners lived permanently in lycra. There were no banks or money exchanges in Muron, you had to bring it with you or in the case of the Australian contingent that I became friendly with, it arrived with a military escort from Moscow.

To get on well with Australians, you have to give them as good or better than you receive. They call you Pommies to start with, then attack the English cricket team, not realising that they don't have a great following, especially among cyclists or footballers. I helps if you know their country, I know a little having spent two extended trips there. In a last resort, if you are losing the debate, you have to remind them that they are all descended from convicts.

In France, Parisienne's are not very well liked outside Paris; the fiercely independent Bretons are more genuine. All the French will agree fonctionnaire's (autocratic officials, there are many in France} are bad news.

On the East Algarve where I live in the winter, the Algarvians think they live in paradise on earth. They talk too loudly, despite this, they accept things they should not, they have allowed the Northerners mostly from Lisbon or Porto to control the most profitable businesses. They could consider taking a leaf from the French, even magistrates and judges manifest in the streets against criminals; sorry, I mean the government.

The Americans, including my second wife who was born in Des Moines, USA, do not want to go back to the USA. The numbers have swelled greatly since the Trump Era.

The Spaniards have lost it: Like Bojo.

The Chinese are taking control of the world. Their tourists who rudely dominate the tourist sites have had the brakes applied for the moment with the Covid-19 pandemic; they will be back in even bigger numbers like a swarm of fire ants.

Sorry, I am supposed to be writing about cycling; but more than that, cyclists. Back to the Oz at Muron. There were 10 to 15 of them that had decided to pool their money. When it arrived, they were rather taken aback by the sheer quantity of notes, which was of course in roubles, there was no chance whatsoever of obtaining other currencies. They had to pile the notes up in the middle of the room on tables, then bring more tables to accommodate it all; that what happens with inflation. Prepare yourselves, there is a high chance it is going to happen to us in the future, how else do you get rid of all the debt? I have no idea what they did with this money; one possibility was to take up the offers of the ladies who were forever calling you on the hotel telephone whatever the hour. Not that I am suggesting that any of them did, I do not have any knowledge as to this. No doubt, these same ladies had established a good trade with the dignitaries who normally stayed at this hotel, visiting the chemical works and surrounding factories. If these telephone calls had not produced results, one would suppose the ladies would stop making them.

It was a big surprise to see the substantial number of religious buildings in the area; the local guide book claims there were 46. Mostly quite splendid looking buildings; some with gold-coloured minarets, many towers of different sizes shapes and colours. My home town of Swinton, a town with a population of 10,000 has many chapels of various denominations and at least one church. None can compare architecturally with any of the churches I saw in Muron at least from the outside, in this atheist country. Bob and myself after a training ride were returning to Muron one day when we were caught in a heavy rain deluge. Spying through the trees, an important looking church we sheltered ourselves and the bikes in the entrance porch against the torrent. After a while, hearing some activity, curiosity propelled us to look inside; where it was very dim with many icons lining the walls and mainly old people swinging incense burners; no one spoke to us. Coming outside, we were accosted by a youngish tall thin woman, speaking very sternly in perfect English, who told us that we should not commit sacrilege by leaving our machines in such a posture in the church entrance porch. Dumbfounded, we left as quickly as we could, without a word.

Meals were conveniently arranged to the departure time of the races where the service could not be faulted. The actual food was another thing; breakfast, noon and night, the same awful grisly meat with rice, almost always the same without fail. This explained to me why there were not many Europeans competing, they had their card marked preferring to give the whole thing a miss. Their lack of numbers was more than made up for by the sheer numbers of Australians and Americans, including women. Understandably, there were plenty of communist country competitors, including of course the Russians themselves. I must have had a premonition as to the food as I had taken with me a well-known brand of a food supplement which had been donated to me. The American ladies had the answer to the food problem. At first, I thought they were running a kindergarten with all the bottles and powders they were mixing, but no, there were no children. They were not going to take them to Russia or perhaps they did not receive visas. For once, it was American intelligence being put to good use in the nutrition department.

The overall winner of each age category was for points gained in each individual event. These events were: One kilometre timed, a timed hill climb, a time trial, a criterium, a road race, an obstacle course, finally a marathon road race. You can see from this it was a very full program. The first event the timed kilometre I did not know where I finished, it could not have been very good as I did not receive a result. Next was the time trial which I won to the annoyance of the American who had won the kilometre. I was third in the criterium. The road race was held on a tricky sporting course in the rain, with diesel spilt on the road, which you had to watch out for. This was my second win. Immediately I rode back to the hotel, where the woman on the desk at the end of the corridor was waiting, as was fashionable in Russian hotels. She did not bat an eyelid when I walked by her in a filthy state, bike and all. In the room I went straight into the shower to wash the dirt and diesel off the bike and myself. The shower was quite efficient, the red bricks walls of the shower did not look any different when I emerged, both the bike and me were shiny and clean. Next was the obstacle course, for which I was able to do some practice using my mountain bike shoes with the VTT cleats. I had the thumbs up from the judge so I must have been OK. After that was the Hillclimb where I hit head on a rider coming down the hill, I must have taken too tight a line on a bend. Before I could recover my wits, if I ever had any, I was in the ambulance. Very quickly I escaped to recover my bike this was not a forgone conclusion even with the permanent Soviet army armed guard that always looked after your bike. Recovering my machine, I persuaded them to let me do a re-run. Having received two winning trophy's and two for third place I thought I must be in the lead, I never had confirmation of this or had sight of any points table. Finally, it came down to the 180 Km. marathon road race where everyone started together. This was very much in my favour as I had plenty of experience in the very similar French Cyclo-Sportives. The main thing to do is to make sure you do not crash, another difficulty in this area of Russia was that the road edge was not straight but rather wavy. Unusually for me in this type of race I lost contact with the lead group. Since I have been a veteran, distance has never been a problem as I have been doing the training and eating correctly. Not only did I lose some ground but had cramp as well. However, I persevered finally getting over it, attaching to a strong group who rode very hard kilometre after kilometre. After a very long chase we were back near the front again. Halfway into this race I never saw any of my competitors, the nearest to me was an Australian who I was sure was well behind. Finally, I crossed the line in a group of young riders with my arms aloft in victory. It was utter chaos at the finish the judges thinking the Australian had finished before me thus giving him the victory. He knew otherwise, sportingly conceding that the judges needed to regard the photo finish – equipment which they did, acknowledging it was me crossing the line with my arms aloft. Fortunately, they reversed the decision, but it was an uncomfortable moment.

In the evening the closing ceremony was rather like the opening one, afterwards we adjourned to the indoor sports hall for drinks and prize presentation. First the ladies received their awards where an American threw a tantrum when she learned that she could not be presented with a rainbow jersey, because there were not enough countries represented in her category. The Russian jersey unlike the western one had a yellow background to the rainbow stripes; I was surprised it was not a red background. For my award I received a jersey that was much too big for me, they had anticipated a Russian winning it, he was seated nearby with a sour puss face. In addition, I received a mound of boxes all filled with Hewlett Packard equipment and computers, I was aware that this was the best of equipment, even better than that I had in my offices. Not that I was an expert on computers, preferring to see my clients face to face, letting others sitting in the office, look at computer screens. The local school to whom I presented the whole bag of mashing's were absolutely delighted. I had no wish to take up their offer of returning for their annual graduation ceremonies.

The return home together with a bus full of other Western riders was a leisurely affair. This was theirs best efforts at introducing us to Russian culture, stopping at some specially programmed events at destinations they thought would interest tourists. For our part all we wanted to do was go home. The coach on arrival at Moscow pulled in front of the big old-fashioned well-known hotel which you often saw on your television screens. Here we were to stay the night before catching our flights back home. The person in charge of the bus asked us all to stay on the coach until it was safe to go into the hotel. Of course, this was all bull shit, so descending the bus everybody had a look in the entrance hall of the hotel. This was quite amazing; it was the size of Piccadilly station, where previously an army of clerks all installed in booths were ready to take your details, as in the days when you had an escort wherever you were to go. They did not need our details, they already had them from the moment we arrived at Moscow airport, if not before. This palaver at this hotel was ridiculous as at Moscow airport by this time, you could book into a hotel exactly as you do in the West. One wonders why Jack did not receive his visa, was this some sort of throwback to their sensitivities as to the area of our destination. Perhaps they thought Jack was a danger, as undoubtedly, they would have learned something of his skills in his precision workshop, where he had a large skilled staff.

Investec Stage Race South Africa 1993

After I won the world championship in Russia, I had an invitation to ride the Investec 4-day stage race in South Africa. You can guess I accepted like a shot, there were two separate races, one for the over 35s, and one for the over 45s, where I was a one-man team. There was a British team in the over 35s which was run separately, apart from the time trial. On arrival at Johannesburg Airport, we were taken direct to a hotel in East Transvaal, now Mpumalanga, I was travelling with my first wife Janet. This area was stunningly breathtaking; it was the location for several films, including, King Solomon's Mines, which is one very old one I can recall. From Gods Window, nearby, a world-famous lookout point, you could look straight down 3000 feet to the plateau of the Lowveld (lower plateau), this then was the backdrop to the race. Mostly, the population were black, very sociable and quite friendly, seemingly very well treated in this area; however the baboons, which we saw everywhere were not to be trusted. The Afrikaner's who made up a good proportion of the population were rather sterner looking, but friendly underneath.

One difference to European racing, time trialling apart, was because of road limitations; we had dead turns in the road, these were well organised and marshalled, as was everything else. The first stage was really hot and humid; at one stage in an isolated forest road, I was out of touch with the leaders, having no legs and really struggling. The day was saved, perhaps more than that, with a sudden lifesaving tropical rainstorm. Later, I was told that the big eagle I had seen following me, was a crowned eagle, quite a big nasty brute and dangerous. Further, I was advised that I was suffering from altitude sickness, nothing worse than that, as the East Transvaal plateau is at an average of 6000 ft. After this stage, I settled in and was back to my usual self, the time trial was my best result and I was only a few seconds slower than the noted tester Ken Platts, being quicker than the rest of the British team.

Later, the organisers complained to me of the poor performance in the race overall of two of the British team, asking if I could explain the reason. I preferred to say that they had been feeling unwell; the truth being that the two in question intended to retire at the end of the season. On receiving such an attractive invitation, these two started training again, but rather late in the day. After the time I had lost on the first stage, the best I could achieve was winning the over 50 classifications. Surprising myself, I finished in front of Nigel Dean in a sprint finish, he was riding in a Zimbabwean team, when I told him, "I was quite pleased as I never thought I would beat you in a sprint finish;" his reply was, "Living out here, you cannot do the same training."

Afterwards, we hired a car, taking an unforgettable two, weeks touring holiday. Before setting off, several of the South

Africans came to us giving their addresses and telephone numbers, saying if you have a problem do not hesitate to give us a call. OOH! The only uneasy night we had was at the hotel near a bus terminal, before we arrived at a small town called St Lucia, not a long way from the Mozambique border. Before this, we had spent four days staying within the renowned Kruger National Park, being free to explore as we wished, before returning to the Park Lodge, which was very civilised. We were out at dawn every day, this being a good time to see the abundant wildlife. Kruger is famous for the big five, Lion, Elephant, Buffalo, Rhino and Leopard, but some of the other animals and birds were equally interesting; it was very dry. One day, there was a brief shower, and the tortoise came out on to the road licking up the water.

After this, it was on to St Lucia, where on the road into the village, we were met by several intimidating looking groups, carrying placards reading **MANDELLA IN WHITES OUT.** Thankfully, they let us pass; the town had all the appearance of a small prosperous Florida vacation town. Stopping at a Pizzeria for a meal, we saw a photographic display of cyclists; on learning I had just ridden the Investec stage race, the waitress rang the owner who arrived immediately with his wife, resulting in us spending the rest of the afternoon drinking an abundant supply of rosy wine. Eventually, indicating we had to leave and find somewhere to stay, they said, "Oh no! You are staying with us." It transpired they had bought the business, private house, furniture, bedding, cutlery, absolutely everything lock stock and barrel, even the drinks were still in the drink's cabinet. The previous owner had fled the country in a panic, fearing what the placards said and what the placard brandishers were hoping, for and what they thought they were voting for. This proved not to be the case, **fortune favours the brave**; the new owners had the bargain of a lifetime.

Afterwards, it was on to Durban and Natal, with driving and staying in the Drakensburg Mountains, before arriving back in Johannesburg. Once there, it was arranged that we stayed with a British Expat in the very large well-known residential area on the outskirts, surrounded by barbed wire, with enough fortifications to stand a siege. Unfortunately, we never went into Joburg; our hosts thought it too risky for us.

Many of the people we meet, indicated it was 9 out of 10 for East Transvaal but 10 out of 10 for Cape Town. Taking the advice, we spent a holiday there five years later, hiring a car, no bikes. New Year's Eve was very special; spending an unforgettable day in the magnificent villa of Bob Theis's international cycling friends, with a swimming pool overlooking Cape Town. To them, we will be eternally grateful. Later, we saw penguins, drove the magnificent world-renowned garden route, I climbed Table Mountain while Janet went up on the cable car. Visiting Stellenbosch, I was able to renew my taste for the very excellent Pinotage wine.

I would give Cape Town 9.5 out of 10, but the visit to the Transvaal was something else, and cannot be repeated, I am told if you want to go there now, you need to travel in a group.

Dinnington Club Life

After becoming more serious when I joined the Dinnington, I was in the favourable position of being able to train in the daytime. Additionally, I did the evening chain gang with my Dinnington Club mates from Doncaster. This was not without its hazards, no V-bombers overhead by now. Having stones thrown at us in the dark, was another early season obstacle. This happened when we passed the gypsy encampment; the youngsters from this camp thought it very amusing. The only way to avoid this was by changing the route; not very easy, when we wanted the benefit of the street lighting as much as possible. Worse than this was, when most in our group were locked in the police cells for the night. It happened one night at the end of our mid-week chain gang, when we were almost home. As we came down the old A1 from Woodlands into Doncaster, just before the north bridge, an accident occurred with a car. I had dropped off the back of the group ready to turn right at Sprotborough traffic light, when I saw, a car driving erratically trying to overtake the group instead of waiting; I did not make the turn but followed as I was concerned as to what might happen. Next, I saw someone had been knocked off, with the car stopped, surrounded by riders. No doubt, the driver was receiving some abuse. Next, the car reversed into the bus that was stopped behind, hitting Mark's bike, he was the one that had been knocked off. There was some damage to the bus; it was at this moment, a pile of drunks alighted from the bus, adding to the general mayhem, just like a scene form Monty Python. Then a solitary policeman appeared, I told him things were not as bad as they appeared, explaining that the drunks had been on the bus. The drunks disappeared into thin air, seeing that Mark was ok, and I could contribute nothing, I too disappeared home.

Next day, I learned that the rest of the peloton had spent the night in police cells. Only Rodger had been released early; Rodger being the legal beagle in the town's litigation department, he no doubt could spin a good tale, as well as a good wheel. Eventually, when the case came to court, the car driver as happens all too often, walked away from the hearing scot-free. Mark and Paul receiving fines. I was never interviewed or called as a witness. We were to learn more than a year later, that this innocent young driver had the book thrown at him for another incident, receiving a long ban.

As the year progressed, my club had a group of riders under the tuition of Alan Geldard (a medal winner at the Melbourne Olympics), training at the Fallowfield track at Manchester to try to win the National Team Pursuit Championship. This entailed travelling on an evening over the Pennines, riders were collected at various points, then all travelling together. As you would imagine, there was not much time to spare. One particular evening when Wayne Randal (a medal winner at the Commonwealth Games in Auckland) was being picked up, he was not quite ready. He explained, "You will have to wait until my brother returns from his paper round as he has my pursuit wheels in his bike."

They had to wait for the return of these expensive wheels shed with silk tubulars, that Wayne had been loaned. It was not recorded how many punctures they had in these special wheels; no doubt Dave Marsh, who had gone to a lot of trouble to obtain these wheels for the use of the club, had good reason not to be very pleased when he learned of this. They eventually qualified for the semi-finals; this is as far as they went.

For my part, I rode the usual races, one of which was an evening circuit race on my doorstep at Brodsworth. In this race, there was a prize for the first veteran which usually Gaz Hill claimed. Not one year because I was able to jump on the wheel of a young up and coming Russ Downing (later to be a National Road Race Champion and Sky rider) hanging on for a few laps until the finish to claim the prize. I knew a good wheel when I saw one. At the age of 58 years, I did even better to win an open promotion by Duncan Ward in the Isle of Axeholm; needless to say the terrain was not too difficult. Les West (infamously beaten into second place in the World Road Race Championship by a doped rider) was another one who could win open events at this sort of age. Very difficult circuits did not bother him; he was to win many open events as a veteran; I was well short of his standard.

Back in Brittany, it was a different story for me, as I gradually became more selective in the races I wanted to ride in. The first one I concluded was too hard for me was at Treveneuc, this went up a long hill, which became steeper at the finish line at the top, then dropped down gradually to the start of the hill with no flat whatsoever. As the years went by, the number of laps I completed became less and less, until I gave up trying to complete this race altogether. My club, the

Velo Club de Quintin, organised many of the races in the villages around the town-Le Foeil, Le Vieux-Bourg, Plelo these were some of them. Another was at St Donan, often in these villages, the circuits together with the starts and finishes were subject to change. Now, the last one I ever rode was at St Donan; in this particular year, the race started in the village itself, at the bottom of a steep hill with a very long drag to the top. Not surprisingly, at the end of the first lap, when I came round to the finish, I was off the back. To my organising colleagues, this was not something they were familiar with, consequently, they demanded to know what the problem was. When I explained that I could not get into my stride with a start up a steep hill like that, they had the answer, that they would change the start for the following year. This was very noble of them; however, we all know that you cannot defy age or gravity. Perhaps, nowadays, you can for a while with an electric bike. There was racing for veterans in my area of France, this was with a different organisation UFLOP, as was veterans racing in the UK, mostly organised by different bodies. The major difference in my experience, was that everyone was welcome in the LVRC in the UK, not so in France, the ex-independents and professionals did not seem to be always welcome. Certainly, my club, admittedly a different organisation, kept mum about these competitions.

Back home, the Mad Hatter was still looking for the magic formula that would help his performance. On visiting the wholesaler merchants who supplied his pet shop, he gave particular scrutiny to the doggy bars that many dogs owners bought for their pets. He discovered a bar with a list of ingredients like the energy bars that many of us ate racing and training, excepting these bars were much cheaper. Dereck found the bars most satisfactory; very soon, the same bars became very popular for many of us. It was not just a question of price; everyone who tried them found them really good. Even Kevin Dawson ate these bars in the 12-hours event. when he won the BBAR (British Best All Rounder for the uninitiated), I don't know which time it was, as Kevin seemed to have laid permanent claim to this competition; no doubt he also ate them in his many road racing exploits. Given the popularity of these bars, it was clear that Dereck's stock could not last forever. On visiting the wholesaler, he was to learn that they were out of stock, they were not buying them anymore because **THE DOGS DID NOT LIKE THEM.**

Klagenfurt Tourist Games, Deutschlondsberg and St Johann Austria

Owning a travel agency sometimes has unexpected advantages, no more so than, when the Austrian Tourist Board, thought up the idea of having their version of a sports games every four years, for workers in the travel industry, a miniature Olympic Games. Some would say, as it was for workers, I should not have qualified, which just goes to show, jealousy compels some to discredit the work that goes into running a cycling training camp. The idea being, this would be a means of promoting the advantages of Austria as a sporting destination. Cycling was one of the major sports they wished to promote. Travel agents were asked to nominate suitable staff for the various sports; it was not a difficult decision to nominate myself for the cycling, no one in our agency dared suggest anyone else.

There were three cycling events, a road race, a time trial and a mountain bike cross-country event. I decided to miss the mountain bike event as I thought transporting one bike would suffice. Luckily, I was selected for the first two; so it was off again, this time with my wife Janet. First, we flew to

Vienna, then it was a small 12-seater aircraft that flew us spectacularly through the mountains to Klagenfurt. The bike went overland as there was not enough space on the aircraft. Klagenfort in Carinthia, turned out to be a super destination, situated on one of the largest and warmest lakes in Europe. Competitors of all ages were from many worldwide destinations, mostly from Europe. Racing was not categorised into age groups, everyone started together in the road race. Equipment was as good as you would see anywhere, excepting for the bike of the Belgium who was the that country's answer to Graeme Obree; his equipment made the Obree creations look high tech. Well, it worked for him; he demoted me into second place by 1.5 seconds. Then, we came to the road race, no one was in the slightest concerned when he disappeared up the road on his own: No one thought he would be any good, on what was a tough mountainous course, on a ridiculously over geared and uncomfortable machine. He completely astounded us as we never set eyes on him again until the finish. Bruno, the Italian known to everyone outsprinted me for second place; he had also won the mountain bike race. Still not bad, a silver and bronze medal, specially minted for the occasion by the Austrian mint.

Myself, Janet and everyone were royally treated for the whole of the week, by the local mayor, tourist board and other dignitaries. The beer and wine had been flowing freely in every sense, the whole of the week. It needed some discipline to actually be fit to compete in the various events. If only more events were like this, but perhaps it is as well they were not, as most likely my life expectancy would have been shorter.

Klagenfurt is a super resort with its Mediterranean climate, sporting opportunities, sightseeing, boutiques and night life; I can certainly recommend it as a holiday destination. At the end of the week, we were additionally treated to the bonus of a tour to visit the Grossglockner Glacier, with an overnight stay on route to the airport at Vienna. As far as I know, the event was never repeated. I suppose it was too costly for the benefits gained, or the tourist board had their budgets cut. The reception given, was at least comparable with the reception given by the host nations at the Association of British Travel Agents conferences, which were held in a different country every year; these while good value for money could be costly. At least, when the conference was in Australia at Surfers Paradise, the Australian government were persuaded to introduce charter flights, everyone gaining as a result. In Austria, I doubt if the gain was very substantial, except for us the participants.

Later at the age of 60, I was to return again to Southern Austria to the Deutschlandsberg cycling week. This was held in the Styria area of Austria with its magical lakes and mountains near the border with Slovenia. This was conveniently arranged the week before the annual Veterans World Championships at St Johann, further to the north in the Austrian Tyrol. The climate in each area was completely different, one to the other. As I described at Klagenfurt earlier, the southern Austrian climate was warmer and more reliable. It could vary from very cold and wet, even misty in the Tyrol to quite hot. Even Jack Wright, again my travelling companion, who unlike me had previously visited St Johann several times, preferred the DLBG climate. Many of the competitors participated in the races at both destinations. My target was the over 60 road races at DLBG.

In this race, I felt extremely good, perhaps it was easier because I was accustomed to racing with younger riders. Half way into the race, I was in a break with six other riders, along with one other rider, we were stronger than the other four, when a break came in our line out, we kept going. The finish was an uphill drag steeper at the top, where I just rode away from my companion. I must have looked fairly fresh; looks can be deceiving as two of the finishing line judges remarked I did not look 60. They must have had the opportunity to check my age with my license, nothing more was said, except congratulations we will see you next year.

Two days later, there was the cyclo-sportive competition, where the choice was either 130 km or 60 km. Both Jack and myself felt a mere 60 km was not worth the effort, as I had never ridden in one so short before, we both opted for the 130 km event. When we arrived at the start-line, we were surprised to see that there were no older riders, everyone looked very youthful; well at least in comparison with us. Soon, I was to find my optimism after my success two days earlier was very misplaced, when we found how hard it was. Unlike at St Johann or at other cyclo-sportives, the roads did not go through the passes in the mountains, but straight over the top. It turned out to be the hardest sportive I had ever ridden. Jack persisted for some time, but discretion was the better part of valour in the end. His race at St Johann was earlier in the week than mine, we were in different age categories, making his abandonment sensible. Many of the younger riders also abandoned, I struggled on finishing about 30 minutes behind the leaders.

At St Johann, it teamed it down with rain all day for my race. Making matter worse, I failed to negotiate the bend in the wet with the front of the bunch, that I had been warned about. This was immediately after the start at the bottom of the climb. Then, I spent all day chasing, even though I felt good, but not succeeding in recovering the ground lost on the bend. It is possible that the sportive had taken an edge off my form; I cannot blame that for a lack of a result. On arrival, wet cold and soggy at our lodgings near the finish, I was locked out of the bedroom with only access to the corridor. As I was frozen to say the least, all I could do was wrap myself in a carpet until someone arrived. Later, when I was somewhat recovered, I went with Jack for a drink in the town bar. On engaging in conversation with another competitor of about my age, who had ridden the same event, I remarked that I was glad it was all over. "Not for me," he replied, "**I have to go and collect my father,** who at this moment is competing in this afternoon race."

Klagenfurt and last races

It was over for me as this was my last international competition, not necessarily because I was 60, but because I did not think I could perform as I would have wished. For different people, retirement comes at different times; there is no set age; it is just a question of how you feel. 31 October 1998 was my last competitive event; this was the Sebastian Hinault's gentlemen's two-up invitation time trial. Sebastian no relation to the other Hinault, Bernard, was a respected professional in the Credit Agricole team for 10 years; the team that was the meal ticket for Chris Boardman. All the Breton pros participated in this event, along with other past and present co-equippers of Sebastian, including the Paris-Roubaix winner Frederic Guesdon. My partner was not a pro, but a very good cyclo-cross rider from Normandy, Cyril Prise.

The 28 km circuit was two laps around what is now my home village of Plouhas. Many of the invitees sat on their partners wheel, enjoying the slip stream, some like our team worked together, enabling us to finish third fastest. This result was very slightly tampered by the fact that Raymond Gautier riding with Stephen Heulot finished second. He had been trying for the last four years to beat me without success, I had not been his favourite person since 1961, when competing in the Rik Van Steenburgen track meeting at Quintin, I had called him some nasty names when he stupidly rode road cranks on this slightly banked track, causing a crash. As justice would have it, he came off worse with a broken collar bone; thankfully, no one else was badly hurt. After a well lubricated three-hour meal, Raymond was feeling chuffed with himself with the results of the racing, buying me a drink; as if I had not already drunk enough.

No More Racing

Cyclo-Tourists in Brittany

No that's not the end of this hotch pot of a rambling rant about days gone by, a whole new world opened to me when I joined the cyclos. Until I retired from racing, I had no idea of a world that existed on a Sunday morning in France. Quite simply when you race at 2.00-3.00 pm. on Sunday afternoon, you are unaware of what happens on a morning. There are many more people with cyclo-touring licenses than there are with racing licenses. In France, there are 3,100 cyclo-touring clubs with 120,000 licensed members. In Brittany alone, there are 340 clubs with 43,210 licensed members.

Many clubs have a printed list and information on the computer, of the routes available for the organised runs. These runs will range in distance from 50 km to 130 km; there will be a program of runs throughout the year, the distance depending on the time of year. All clubs would have a Sunday morning run, plus one or two runs during the week; most club members would be retired, these members would mostly do the mid-week runs; the working members would only participate in the Sunday runs. The number of members would influence the number of runs on the day in question, a club with 200 licenses may have four runs on a Sunday; a club with 20 members would probably have only one. The mid-week runs would be either on a morning or in the afternoon, depending on the time of the year; the Sunday runs would always be on a morning. Departures would be prompt, no waiting around. In addition to runs solely for members, most clubs organise randonais open to other clubs on a Sunday morning, most often with a meal afterwards. As there are very many cyclo-clubs in Brittany, without travelling too far, you could ride a different circuit and meet different people as often as you would wish. A distinct advantage in Brittany, apart from scenic and varied terrain is the absolute fantastic network of traffic-free smaller roads, especially on a Sunday morning. VTT (mountain biking) clubs are also very popular. In the winter months or any time of the year, if you want a change, you could ride with a mountain bike club at the weekend. They also organise randonais in the winter, just like the cyclos with a meal afterwards. Again, you would be able to find a good one, without travelling too far.

After an initial trial with a couple of clubs, I finally joined the Cyclo Club Plouhatin. They were the third largest club in the Cotes D' Armor with 150 licenses, there were several groups in this club, as you would expect with a club of this size. It is almost 100% the case, when a license is held that they ride a bike; people don't take a license solely to say, they belong to this or that club. At the time of joining, we had a house in Plourhan, six km from Plouha, the village of my new club, which was built for us in the year 2000. After my permanent retirement, we moved to a bigger house in the village centre at Plouha, where we could walk to the local shops and even the local bar, where we met after the club runs.

Plouha has a population of 4,000 with 2,000 in the village and another 2,000 in the countryside, or directly on the coast.

We have the highest cliffs in Brittany. We live three km from the nearest beach, having five in total; two are blue flag beaches ones at the time of writing in 2020. The most famous one is the Plage Bonaparte where 135 airmen of several nationalities, who had crashed in France, having escaped the Nazis, were repatriated to England. These airmen were rescued and taken care of by the Resistance, during the period 1943-44 and subsequently taken to Plouha. It was at this plage, at that time named L'Anse Cochat, where the extremely courageous resistance cell known as the Shelburn Cell, escorted these airmen on the darkest nights at great risk to themselves to the waiting Royal Navy. This is depicted in a film of 2019 called ALLO CINE which immortalises the Resistance Shelburn and the brave men and women of this group. The port of Gwin Zegal, also part of Plouha, is also classified as a site remarkable, it is one of the only two ports of its type in France, where the boats are moored to poles fixed to the seabed.

If I thought I had done with competition, I was mistaken, as very many of the group one runs resembled a race, with no stops, very unlike UK club runs. Most members arriving back in Plouha at the same time, other groups a little later at the same bar; the slowest group often did a shorter route, arriving at a similar time to the rest of us. With many of us meeting in the same bar after the runs, this became our headquarters and was very convivial indeed. Once a month, I introduced a British style club run for the day. To attract a good following, I had to find a very good restaurant, at a modest price for lunch. I organised these runs taking a long way round to the restaurant, with a shorter mileage back home to Plouha. The average distance was about 150 km. Often, during the year, we organised a 3-or 4-day touring trip with a following vehicle to carry our belongings, which was also useful in case of problems. Over the years, we had some spectacular trips to many very different regions, France is a magnificent country for cycle touring, with a breath-taking variety of terrains without equal.

A unique experience was a tour to Paris, finishing with a private motorcycle escort the Sunday morning, shepherded by the Guard de la Republic (the president of France's personal motorcycle escort). We did all the sights at a leisurely pace, the Eiffel Tower, Bois de Boulogne, left bank of the Seine, Versailles, etc. Among the brief stops we had, was a stop at the Palace of Versailles, with its horde of tourists. Our club clothing was by chance red, white, and blue, I overheard one tourist remark, "Oh, **look it is a group of the minister for sport**." Even I knew at that time it was a lady who was the female minister (Femme Ministre). This chance of a lifetime came about because we had a recently retired police inspector from Paris join our club. His friend was the captain in charge of the president's motorcycle escort, who gave up their spare time to orchestrate our group. Of course, the traffic was less dense on a Sunday, but still busy enough; it was absolutely necessary to have a strict control if any motorist moved an inch, they had a shrill whistle warning, rooting them to the spot for fear of retribution. We were very fortunate to have this privilege and unforgettable once in a lifetime experience.

We have had many visits to the southwest of France, where my friend Loic Burvingt has a property in Saint Cyprien. As a result, we have close links with the cyclo-club in Saint Cyprien, who have also benefited from visiting our area. Loic is the very efficient and consciences organiser of many of our club cycling holidays. One of our favourite rides from Saint Cyprien is to follow the coast south into Spain. We set off with a gorgeous view on our right of the Catalonian's mythical mountain, Le Canigue, which rises to 2784 meters. On our left, we have the sea, then after passing Argeles Plage, we encounter the never-ending climbs and descents along the coast, giving fabulously unequalled views over the sea and mountains. The route continues passing the tourists favourite destination of the fortified town of Collioure, then it's on to the wine fields of Banyuls, famous for its dessert wines, crossing the Spanish border at Cerbere. We continue along the coast, before finally turning off the Roses Road, towards Figures. It is then back into France at the border town of Perthus.

This route takes us very near Roses, where we have twice enrolled in the Cinquante Trois (53/12) training camps for the 15 days in April. At this camp, we organised our own program, not being part of the camp that organisers highly structured training rides. Consequently, being perceived as touring cyclists which we were, we were not taken seriously. This all changed when the organisers held their hill climb race, climbing up to the Monastir De Sant Pere De Rodes. The veterans and all the ladies on the serious camp, were to start in one group together, at the bottom. Michel Aubree my clubmate, who was still racing at the time entered this competition, being the only entry from our group. It was no surprise, on the day of the race that Michel appeared alone at the top to our waiting ranks. He is one year younger than me and is a past French veteran's road race champion, winning the hill climb race at the World Championships at St Johann. The lady who was second over the line was accustomed to beating the veterans every year. She claimed to have established the time for the fastest lady on this climb, beating the time set by Jeanie Longo. She was quite miffed, to put it mildly, at being beaten by a veteran giving a lame excuse for this, saying she would do a re-ride. She was told she would have to improve considerably, as the Plouhatin Club had a veteran's ex-world champion among their ranks, if he was needed. That shut her up big time, completely changing the attitude towards ourselves. What I could have told them was that Michel was a better climber than I was, but it was better to keep them in the dark.

Roses as a base for training in the winter is very popular with the French, much more so than Mallorca. The advantage for them is, that they can drive there without flying or taking a ferry and that the terrain is very varied. Hotels are of a reasonable standard, as well as being keenly priced. There is also an abundance of apartments to rent in the winter, at low prices. Whilst Roses has its attractions, in my opinion it cannot hold a candle to its near neighbour across the water, Mallorca.

Another very popular destination where my club has organised holidays, is the Var, staying a couple of times at Vaison le Romain. This is a well frequented base for climbing the Ventoux, along with the many well frequented cycling routes in this splendid area. In the town, we successfully listed the help of the local cycling club, to show us the best back roads to ride. Later in the week, we were invited to join them on the Sunday, when they had a specially organised a ride into the mountains. Being the only one from the Plouha club accepting this invitation, I went along to the town to meet them for the start. The surprise awaiting me was that only the younger club members were there, the rest had travelled by car a further 30 km to make the day easier. We joined up with them later. After some hard terrain at the top of a long hard climb, I saw the sign at the top which read, Col de L' Homme Mort 1212 m (Dead Man); no doubt, there was more than one dead man, as there was only four of us left. The four of us pressed on alone, as one remarked you must ride at your own pace on these climbs, so it is pointless waiting for the stragglers. After five cols., the one rider who was slightly the strongest of the four, asked if anyone wanted to make the last climb the Ventoux. It was out of the question for me, I had ridden the climb earlier in the week, that was enough. I did not have any desire to finish up joining Tom, there would have been no monument erected to me on the mountain. As no one else volunteered to join him, he continued to ride the Ventoux alone. It was three hours later when I saw him again, after I had a shower and a meal. It was on leaving the restaurant, I saw this brave or more likely, this foolish rider, just about crawling back home, one climb too many for him. The day after, the only time in my life I have ridden six cols. in one day, I set off with my clubmates on a rather easy modest ride. Soon, I found I had a sore knee and had to return to the holiday village where we were staying. After a further day's rest, my knee was ok and I was back to normal, if I ever am normal.

Another year also at Vaison le Romain, we had an invitation to attend a welcoming buffet at the local Presbytere, (Vicarage). This came about because the Vicare (the assistant to the curate) was well known to at least one of our members, where he occupied this same position as at Plouha, having just been transferred to Vaison Le Romain. On arriving at the Presbytere, this was very modest looking from the outside, even the entrance was somewhat dilapidated; however, once inside, the difference was quite noticeable. To welcome us, there was a very long table with a very good selection of various edibles with wide variety of wines, beers and liqueurs to wash all the food down. There might have been soft drinks or water as well, but if there was, I did not notice. A very sociable afternoon was enjoyed by all, even the jokes by our friend the Vicare were amusing, which is not always the case with French jokes. Here is one of the jokes he told, this is partly in Breton, I will not translate this, neither will I make any other comment, except to say it was not the most amusing. Here, it is for you to judge for yourselves, if you so desire, sorry I cannot print the accents.

Dans une église de Pont L'Abbe
Une bonne dame avait pete
La cure lui dit:
Votre cucul sere cousu.
Ma doue Koulzkoudi Monsieur Le Cure
Qu'il ne soit que faufile

To continue my brush with religion, we had a cross-country tour where on the last day, we rode up the Tourmalet, when it was 30 degrees. The night before our hotel was conveniently situated at Lourdes, where I was reluctantly persuaded to visit the pilgrimage site with my friends. They told me it is an experience; you must come; indeed, it was, I never expected it to be so commercial. On arriving back in Plouha, I was asked if I had drunk the holy water in the fountain. "No," I replied, "definitely not." I saw the pigeons making a special effort to ***direct their droppings into the fountain.***

Another big cyclo-tourism occasion in France, indeed the biggest, is the Semain Federal, which is often held in the hottest part of France the first week in August. This takes much organisation, as there are often 10,000 license holders taking part who need accommodation; most stay on the organised camp sites, a few in hotels; many more stay in private accommodation. The local inhabitants are persuaded to open their homes for the week. There is a choice of routes and distances every day, with detailed maps, food and drink stops are widely organised; there are at least three fully operational sites on the route with music, different displays of local handicrafts, foodstuffs, first-aid facilities and much more. Many British also participate, including usually a big group from the Concord Club in Birmingham. The Verdun event was sadly the last one for Bob Maitland. One afternoon I went round to the campsite to see him, the first person I saw was Jill Lloyd, saying, "Bad news, Gordon, Bob collapsed this morning at the Permanence (headquarters) and was taken to hospital." From the local hospital, he was taken to Montpellier where he died several days later; regrettably one occasion where we did not meet.

Winter Riding in Portugal's Algarve

Since 2005, I have spent the winter in Tavira, East Algarve, Portugal, situated in the Ria Formosa Natural Park. This protected area extends 60 km from Faro in the west, to Cancela in the east. This is a series of pristine natural islands, with extensive saltwater lagoons and tidal mudflats. They are a haven for breeding fish and a bird watcher's paradise, with storks, flamingos, heron, spoonbills among the many species. This stretch of coastline is thus protected from the powerful seas and is much quieter than West Algarve, as the area is not blessed with the plethora of hotels that there are in the west; they are not allowed in this national park. An important reason I came here at the time and not Pollensa, was because it was much livelier here in December and January, the climate being very similar. This nowadays is a very viable cycling alternative to Mallorca, for a start it is not as busy. That is an understatement, there is an excellent network of roads to the north of the coastal 125 road. This main coastal highway is best avoided; you can go for miles on the multitude of minor back roads and the more important roads in the mountains, hardly seeing another vehicle. A baby lynx I recently saw dead at the side of the road, apparently hit by a vehicle, was extremely unlucky. It is a little harder to find flatter roads, but there are many variations of really enjoyable scenic minor roads towards the Spanish frontier, the best roads are without a doubt on the Portuguese side of the border. In the towns and villages, there are a higher density of bars than I have seen anywhere, and the excellent coffee is not expensive. In fact, the French should come to Portugal to learn how to make good coffee.

Flights to Faro Airport are very numerous; Tavira is only half an hour away from the airport. It must be said that cycling is not very organised in the Algarve. Perhaps, this is not true of the mountain biking fraternity as they have some organised mountain bike racing, their clubs are growing in popularity. The terrain and tracks are well suited to mountain biking or gravel riding as many now say, especially my American second wife. You would need to belong to a club to be introduced and get to know the tracks that you could ride, as you would not find them on your own.

Cyclo-tourism is growing in popularity, from small beginnings, unlike France, there are younger riders, who for the most part have expensive machines, but not yet electric-assist bikes. There are several smaller clubs, even a lady's team in Lloule and a professional team in Tavira. Apart from the Tour de Algarve, which attracts the big international teams at the beginning of the season, they race mostly in Spain and the Lisbon area. A feature of the Algarve is the cyclo-randonais event, when the Covid-19 is not around. Normally, there is an event somewhere every couple of weeks, always on the Sunday morning. Usually, you pay 10 euros in total which includes club transport to the event and the meal afterwards. The advantage of the smaller clubs is that there is availability in the club minibus for transport to the event. Assistance is often given by the local council (Junta), towards the purchase of a vehicle.

However, these rando's are not everyone's cup of tea. They are quite unique to the Algarve, in that the bunch starts together and stays together. You all ride behind a lead vehicle which you cannot pass, with motor bike outriders and the police controlling the traffic, either in squad cars or on motorcycles. The disadvantage is that everyone cannot climb at the same pace; on the descents, you must break heavily to let the bunch reform. Sometimes, when the climbs are very challenging, the older riders know to give these circuits a miss. If you like the conviviality and an inexpensive meal with plenty of wine and beer, these events are for you. Be warned however, that the Algarvians are better eaters, especially drinkers, than they are bike riders. Mostly they think that they live in paradise on earth, who could argue, especially now the back roads are tarmacked.

Cyclos Pilgrimage to Fatima

One year along with Woolly Jersey (Tony), Odd Crank (Steve) and the father of Odd Crank, John, we decided to participate in the annual pilgrimage to Fatima with the cyclos of the Algarve. Rather odd for three atheists, which I think includes John; he won't stop talking for long enough to consider the question. This was an organised group, starting in Albufeira, finishing at Fatima, with overnight stops on route with ample food and drinks provided. Jerseys and shorts were a compulsory extra. With the multitude of advertisers crammed on these garments, if I had been paid, as in the old days back in Brittany, of say one euro per km for each sponsor, I would have received a truly princely sum. Instead, we were charged two euros for the privilege of wearing this clothing. Our story is that we were not searching for paradise, but went along for the ride, neither for the almost free cycling attire. All three of us belonged to different clubs in the Tavira area, John was added as a holiday guest for this allegedly, spiritually uplifting adventure.

We were meant to ride all together as one group, which was not easy with the plethora of odd individuals, just like us, of all ages and an array of bicycles of all descriptions, at least our bikes were ok. I would claim no more than this. We started with about 200 riders, a long caravan following, with more police outriders than in the Tour de Algarve. After leaving the urban sprawl of Albufeira, it has grown exponentially since I first went there many years ago, we transgressed the steeply wooded and twisty roads of the Serra De Calerao, passing through Castro Verdie to arrive in the Alentejo. Our destination after 130 km was the village of Aljustrel, which we reached largely intact; no doubt with some divine assistance, for our overnight stay. Seeing the hard floor in the gymnasium, we were meant to sleep in for the night, even though we had sleeping bags etc., I went and found us a hostel that was not as primitive. We all partook of the evening meal arranged in the same gymnasium, retiring on foot, quite happily after eating and drinking plenty, as was the Portuguese habit, to our hostel. My bike joined the two bikes of my Portuguese clubmates Manuel and Esquel in the Mario Concalvez Club vehicle, with whom I had arrived at Albufeira. My three accomplices, I mean companions left their bikes in the gymnasium, along with some of our belongings.

Before I proceed with the story, it will help if I tell you more about my two Portuguese clubmates and friends. Manual went to work in France in the building trade, having been declined for the military when he went to enlist, because as a youngster, he lived in an isolated village in the mountains, never going to school. He is now in his 80s and still goes to night school to improve his English. Well, he progressed in the building trade, as a result of his hard work and endeavours, he now owns seven properties in the Tavira area. Esquel, for his part went to work in South America as a mechanic. On his return to the Algarve, he obtained employment as a KEY

MAN, that is letting people back into their house after being locked out. One day, he had let a young attractive wealthy Madeiran widow, now settled in the Algarve, and himself back into her house, where he remains to this day. Suffice to say these two gentlemen are not dummies. In order to reduce the energy exerted into the ride by half, they had the nuance to share the riding, one would drive, whilst the other would ride. Unfortunately, this arrangement whilst cutting their mileage in half, apparently only increased the stress that they felt.

Next morning, we arrived on foot with our luggage at the previous night's gymnasium, where my three companions' bikes and the rest of our luggage remained. Everybody, belongings and all, had departed to have breakfast in the local school at the other side of the village. Not wanting to drag our luggage through the streets, the obvious thing to do was to ring my clubmate Manual, to ask whoever it was that had decided to drive, to come back to the gymnasium to collect our luggage. Unfortunately, there was no phone signal, Steve was dispatched on his cycle to ask Manual or Esquel to come back to the gymnasium with my bike before they departed, collecting the remaining luggage at the same time. The plan then was to set off independently on our bikes, stopping at one of the bars along the route for breakfast. Then in team pursuit formation, we would re-join the cavalcade, which was well within our capabilities. Steve for his part, had been assiduously studying Portuguese language for the past 10 years, myself I had given up when my Portuguese teacher from Lisbon, admitted that she could not understand the local Algarvians.

On Steve's return, seeing our anxiety, he assured us that Manual had understood our message and he had every confidence in our request being fulfilled. Quite clearly, we could hear the police sirens, as they were obviously preparing to leave. As there was still no sign of Manual or anybody else for that matter, Steve ventured that our rescuing vehicle must be blocked in and would arrive in due course. We were not the only ones who had made other sleeping arrangements the night before, I knew of one other club, where they had booked hotels within driving distance of the start. Certainly, the president and a couple of others from the Algarve Cyclo Touring Federation were booked in the best hotels. There was no chance of them doing otherwise when they could legitimately use their expense accounts to spend the members subscriptions; our situation was not unique. Still, no one appeared after a half an hour's wait, the truth finally dawning on us that we had been abandoned. Luckily, for us, a couple from Lisbon, who had been loosely following the pilgrimage in their camping car, saw our predicament. They very graciously agreed to take me and the luggage to the rear of the pilgrimage cavalcade. The three remaining set off on their bikes, with instructions to look for me having my breakfast in a roadside bar on the route, when I recovered my bike. Then we would all re-join the group together.

Arriving at the cavalcade, fortunately I had a phone signal, it being Manual who answered my call saying, "It's my turn to drive."

"Where is my bike?" I asked.

"It's in the back of the van," he nonchalantly replied, apparently completely unconcerned. "Ok," I said, "I would like you to stop and let me have it," which he did. The nice people from Lisbon were relieved to see the back of me, especially the luggage helping me load it into the van. They then sped off at great speed, in the opposite direction.

Following the plan, I was seated outside of a bar having my second cup of coffee, when one of the police outriders, the GNR branch (Guardia National de Republique), they are made of sterner stuff than the rest, arrived. Their instructions were, "You will have to leave as you must all ride together," to which I replied, "I am waiting for my three friends."

"No, we have collected them," was the reply.

"No, you must have mistaken them with the British from the Portimao Club." At that, he gave up and left. Next a van came by at great speed, screeching to a stop with Steve jumping out whilst it was still moving. He said, "I saw you, but they did not want to stop. What happened was they saw us riding our bikes and insisted, we leave our bikes to come with them in the van," he explained. They claimed that they would send someone else to collect the bikes. Steve refused to leave the bikes in the middle of nowhere unattended. Eventually, another vehicle came back to collect them, which explains why all and sundry were in great haste. Eventually, we all arrived at the destination of Montemor-O-Novo after 139 km. That night, we were accommodated uncomfortably in the sports hall, with everyone else. The next day, we were instructed to ride with the bunch, under threat of excommunication, or worse. After riding with the group like good little boys for the short 85 km, we made it to Alpiarca for the overnight stay. Finally, on the last day, after an early start for the 70 km, arriving just before noon at Fatima. Immediately, my three companions having succeeded in making arrangement to return to Tavira, left with great haste, abandoning me to savour the delights of Fatima. In truth, I was wishing I could also leave but I have no regrets as to staying, as I can now recount my experience of Fatima.

As my two Portuguese clubmates indicated, they were not ready to leave until later, I made use of the time by making a tour of the religious site. All the shops in the town were devoted to selling tatty religious souvenirs, so I had nothing better to do. I was still pretty fresh after the 70 km completed in the morning. Exploring the massive Fatima sight, was very tiring; as a commercial entity, it seemed to me to even dwarf the site at Lourdes. Esquel and Manual indicated that it would be very late when we finally left, I have no idea what they did with their time, perhaps they slept for the first time in four days. Consequently, I agreed with a helper from another club, to go back to the pilgrimage sight with him; so he could very quickly take a few photographs. Then, we would go to a local bar to watch the Portuguese National Football team, who were playing a big match live on TV that night.

However, we made a big mistake, as we could not leave with all the crowds suddenly arriving, blocking the exits. By this time, it was becoming dark, everybody was lighting up the candles they were carrying. This appeared to me to be very dangerous, as with the close proximity of everyone, it was a wonder no one was set on fire. Seeing two ladies with so many candles in each hand, I remarked it was a pity I did not know you when you were younger, all I received in reply was a few giggles. By this time, the barriers were put into place, where the bishops and others were to parade with the cross. I saw one very unfortunate lady, who I had noticed on my earlier visit, was just a few yards short of completing her crawl along the line of repentance, on bare unprotected knees, to the shrine. The erected barriers, where she was clasping the last one, had stopped her progress. She would have to wait for quite some time, till everyone went home and the barriers were removed to complete the last few yards. In her own mind, her sin must have been serious for her to endure this ordeal. The bishops were starting their chants on the newly erected podium; I thought these were only used at bike races. Believe it or not, I saw the absolute double of Victor Meldrew the actor from the Grumpy Old Man series on the TV, perhaps it was him, raise up with his hands in tune with the chants, crying hallelujah hallelujah and then slump back down again. He seemed to be making a big physical effort to be able to do this, then he did not move for quite some time, then recovering to repeat his forlorn cry, over and over. When he remained slumped of the ground for a longer period, I thought he had snuffed it, but he recovered. As the crowd moved towards the podium, we saw an escape route, finally escaping from the maddening throng. Unfortunately, we missed the football. I know not if Victor survived the night, but I saw the real one on TV later, or perhaps it was recorded. No doubt, the lady completed her penance in due course, it is not recorded if she was forgiven her sins.

Later, several days later, I asked Manuel what he was thinking about when he left with my bike, leaving me without any transport. His reply was that it was very stressful for him and Esquel at the time, deciding who was driving and who was riding, it was all he was thinking about, adding, "**WE ONLY WENT TO PLEASE OUR WIVES.**"

Nuts and Bolts

I never kept a diary or made a collection of newspaper cuttings, mostly I have written from memory. The two articles I wrote for the Sporting Cyclist in 1960/61 have been of assistance. In addition, I had kept the race itinerary or program for the Tour de France L'Avenir, the Bayern Rundfahrt, the Investec 4-day stage race, where it is noted that the British team for the separate younger age race was: Keith Gordon, Mark Robinson, Geoff Platts and Phil Galloway. Also, I had the result for the race Tom won on 13 June 1958, plus the souvenir programme for the Vaux Grand Prix 18 June 1967. One program only was kept from the seven times I rode the Tour of Luxembourg, as this was for 1985, it must have been the first time I rode, where the only two other British riders listed were Doug Collins and Denis Hill. Luckily, I retained a copy of the German magazine *The Velo* for 1988, which had some details of the races in Provence, add to the list a couple of French magazines which had cyclo-sportive results. By chance, a couple of years ago I purchased an old *Sport and Vie* magazine in a local bric-a-brac at Binic, which had some details of the Mid Aout Bretagne for 1961.

At one time, I did have a log book of the prize money I had earned recording the finishing results for my time in

Brittany. A necessary check of verification to make sure you received your entitlement.

A few years ago, when I was clearing things out, I came across these records, when looking at the money involved, I was disgusted with how little this was and threw them away. I did not think it so little at the time, it kept the wolf from the door. Supposedly, I have been influenced or even indoctrinated by the earnings of the businesses I have owned and directed. Unquestionably, I was not the biggest earner as a cyclist, but the confidence and experience I gained in the years 1960/61/62, have stood me in good stead in the world after cycling. Thereafter, going on to have a successful business career, even though being hampered by the politics of the time. Some of the most successful riders have made a complete mash of their investments or business endeavours later. Stephen Roche's debts of £730,000 accrued by his hotel and trainings camps in Mallorca has made him no longer welcome on this island. A recent example is Cippolini's restaurant venture in the USA. Earlier Malcolm Elliot's earnings were managed by a broker who misappropriated the funds; Malcolm having a few years of worry before he received compensation. Barry Hoban's venture into the new cycle factory in Wales went belly up, finally working as a rep very successfully at Phil Griffiths Cycle import business, Yellow Ltd. Even Bernard Hinault's investments in cycling component manufacturing and agricultural supplies were said not to have been without problems, which I suppose is why he went to work for the Tour de France at a salary not commensurate with his status. Sir Bradly Wiggins appears to have joined the list with several liquidations of companies he had ploughed money into. Currently, he is being sued for debts in excess of one million pounds.

I did not think you the reader wanted boring with too many details of this and that race. Some time ago, I looked at a book of some lesser rider like me, talking about what gear they rode in this time trial and why they preferred this course to that course, I thought this is so boring; I am trying not to fall into that trap. I hope I have succeeded not just C, and I hope you will understand if an 82-year-old's memory is not perfect.

I have tried not to express any religious or political view having written about events I have actually witnessed, but I have failed by admitting I am atheist and did not vote for Brexit as I consider myself fundamentally a European. I will comment on my opinion of the current situation after Brexit. I believe that for the ordinary citizen it has eroded our rights to benefit from being geographically European. What is not understood is the immigration policy of the UK as opposed to the EU, the UK being far more liberal than the EU in accepting skilled workers on a worldwide basis. if they have the necessary skills…